Green **Line** 3

von
Marion Horner
Elizabeth Daymond
Paul Dennis
Randall Jonas
Andrea Kealey

herausgegeben von
Harald Weisshaar

Ernst Klett Verlag
Stuttgart · Leipzig

Green Line 3 Workbook

für Klasse 7 an Gymnasien und für den Bildungsstandard Klasse 8 in Baden-Württemberg

Herausgeber: Harald Weisshaar, Bisingen
unter besonderer Mitwirkung von Frank Haß, Kirchberg.

Autoren: Marion Horner M.A., Cambridge; Elizabeth Daymond M.A., Kiel; Paul Dennis M.A., Lahnstein; Randall Jonas, M.A., Montreal; Andrea Kealey, Mannheim sowie Peter Lampater, Ehingen

Zeichenerklärung:

- Diese Texte und Übungen sind auf den Schüler- und auf den Lehrer-CDs.
- Diese Übungen / Übungsteile sind Partnerarbeit.
- Diese Übungen / Übungsteile sind Gruppenarbeit.
- Diese Übungen / Übungsteile sind besonders knifflig oder anspruchsvoll.
- Diese Übungen / Übungsteile sind besonders leicht.

1. Auflage 1 5 4 3 2 | 2012 11 10 09 08

Alle Drucke dieser Auflage sind unverändert und können im Unterricht nebeneinander verwendet werden. Die letzte Zahl bezeichnet das Jahr des Druckes.

Internetadresse: www.klett.de

Redaktion: Anette Dangelmaier M.A.

Gestaltung: Anita Bauch; Wiebke Hengst, Ostfildern
Illustrationen: Lars Benecke, Hannover; Naomi Fearn, Berlin sowie David Norman, Meerbusch
Umschlaggestaltung: Koma Amok, Stuttgart
Umschlagfoto: Ariel Skelley / Corbis
Reproduktion: Meyle + Müller, Medien-Management, Pforzheim
Druck: W. Wirtz, Speyer

Printed in Germany
ISBN 978-3-12-547146-7

9 783125 471467

Hi! Ich bin's, Kelsey.
Wie im Schülerbuch sind auch im Workbook einige neue Elemente hinzugekommen, die ich dir kurz erklären möchte.

- Zwischen den beiden *Language*-Teilen gibt es die neue Seite *Talkwise*, in der es ausschließlich um das Sprechen geht.
- In jeder Unit gibt es eine Übung zu *Writing Texts*, die dir hilft, deine Schreibfertigkeiten zu verbessern.
- Auf der *Skills*-Seite in jeder Unit findest du nützliche Tipps zu Lesen, Hören, Schreiben usw.
- Zusätzlich zu den *Skills* innerhalb der Units findest du auf S. 77–82 weitere *Skills*-Seiten. Hier übst du noch einmal intensiv *Listening-*, *Reading-*, *Writing-* und *Project-Skills*. Die wichtigsten Tipps zu den einzelnen Skills sind darin übersichtlich zusammengefasst.

Noch ein paar Worte zur Arbeitsweise mit dem Workbook: Dein Lehrer/deine Lehrerin korrigiert deine Arbeit im Workbook oder ihr besprecht die Übungen gemeinsam im Unterricht.
Die Übungen auf den *Check-out*-Seiten kannst du jedoch selber korrigieren! Die Lösungen zum Überprüfen deiner Ergebnisse findest du am Ende des Workbooks.

Und – *last but not least:* Die folgenden Arbeitsanweisungen werden dir im Workbook immer wieder begegnen. Falls du dir mal nicht ganz sicher bist, was du bei einer Übung machen sollst, kannst du in dieser Liste nachschauen.

Viel Spaß und Erfolg mit **Green Line 3**!

Add the missing words.	Füge die fehlenden Wörter hinzu.
Cross out …	Streiche … durch.
Decide …	Entscheide / Entscheidet …
Draw an arrow.	Zeichne einen Pfeil.
Draw circles round …	Kringle … ein.
Draw lines.	Ziehe / Zeichne Linien.
Fill in … (the grid/the list …)	Fülle … (die Tabelle / die Liste) aus.
Finish …	Stelle … fertig. / Vervollständige …
Go on, please.	Mach' / Macht bitte weiter.
Go on with the answers.	Ergänze die Antworten.
Listen (and write).	Höre zu (und schreibe mit).
Look at the words in brackets.	Schau / Sieh dir die Wörter in Klammern an.
Make a list.	Schreibe eine Liste.
Make questions and answers.	Schreibe Fragen und Antworten auf.
Make sentences …	Bilde Sätze …
Put in …	Setze … ein.
Read … to your partner.	Lies … deinem Partner / deiner Partnerin vor.
Take turns …	Wechselt euch ab …
Talk about …	Spreche / Sprecht über …
Then fill in the speech bubbles.	Fülle danach die Sprechblasen aus.
Underline the words.	Unterstreiche die Wörter.
Use the ideas on the right.	Verwende die Ideen / Angaben auf der rechten Seite.
What are the missing words?	Welche Wörter fehlen?
What are the words?	Welche Wörter sind das?
What is missing?	Was fehlt?
What is right?	Was ist richtig?
Work in a group.	Arbeitet in einer Gruppe.
Work with a partner.	Arbeite mit einem Partner / einer Partnerin.
Write complete sentences.	Schreibe vollständige Sätze.
Write down …	Schreibe … auf.
Write it on the line.	Schreibe es auf die Zeile.
Write the sentences.	Schreibe die Sätze auf.

Unit 1 The world of sport

1 What is wrong here? (→ PB p. 8)

a) *Talk to your partner about the pictures. Say what the sports are and find the mistakes.*

b) *In your exercise book, write down two correct facts for every sport in a).* ***(Erwartungshorizont S. 86)***

2 Listening: Sports news (→ PB p. 9)

Tick ✔ the box with the correct information.

1. The winner of the 100 metres race is …
   a) British champion. ☐
   b) European champion. ☐
   c) world champion. ☑

2. One swimmer …
   a) is 50 metres in front of the others. ☐
   b) is going to win easily. ☑
   c) has already finished the race. ☐

3. The tennis umpire …
   a) thinks the ball landed on the line. ☐
   b) thinks the ball landed outside the court. ☑
   c) is angry with the player. ☐

4. The football player scores the goal …
   a) with her head. ☑
   b) with her hand. ☐
   c) with her foot. ☐

3 Put in the missing words (→ PB p. 8)

1. rugby – grass
   ice hockey – *ice*
2. tennis – umpire
   football – *referee*
3. rugby – pitch
   tennis – *court*
4. ice hockey – stick
   baseball – *bat*
5. foot – boot
   head – *helmet*
6. skateboarding – America
   cricket – *England*
7. basketball – player
   swimming – *swimmer*
8. cricket – hit
   football – *kick*
9. field – game
   track – *race*

4 Complete the information with simple present forms of the verbs (→ PB p. 10)

be 1

start 2

go on for 3

leave 4

1. The next judo competition is on September 8th.
2. The big football match tomorrow starts at 3 pm.
3. The tennis course next month goes on for three days.
4. The train for the rugby fans on Saturday leaves at 9.20.

finish 5

5. The cricket season finishes next week.

5 Write down what everyone is doing next week (→ PB p. 11)

Next week is a special 'keep fit week' for Laura's class. The pupils are doing different activities every day to help their fitness. Use the present progressive to explain what they are doing.

Mon: do aerobics in the break ✓ | Tues: play rugby after school | Wed: go swimming in the afternoon | Thurs: jog round the playground at lunchtime | Fri: have 'crazy sports' competitions all day

1. On Monday they are doing aerobics in the break.
2. On Tuesday they are playing rugby after school.
3. On Wednesday they are going swimming in the afternoon.
4. On Thursday they are jogging round the playground at lunchtime.
5. On Friday they are having 'crazy sports' competitions all day.

6 Make dialogues with your partner (→ PB p. 11)

Grace wants to do things with Jill, but Jill has already made other arrangements for that day.

Example: Grace: Let's go to the skatepark on Friday.
Jill: Sorry, I can't. I'm meeting a friend on Friday.

watch | meet | play | visit | have | ride | help | go

A
Would you like to … / Let's … / Why don't we … / … + on …

B
Sorry, I can't. / I haven't got time. / It's a nice idea, but … / … + I'm … on …

7 Put in the correct tense: Simple present or present progressive (→ PB p. 11)

Sports fans Alex and Danny _are travelling_ (travel) to London together next Saturday. Their train _leaves_ (leave) Leicester at 8.35 am. But the two boys have got tickets for different events, so after their arrival in London they _are doing_ (do) different things. Cricket fan Alex _is watching_ (watch) the England cricket team and tennis fan Danny _is going_ (go) to Wimbledon. Danny has got more time than Alex because the cricket _starts_ (start) at 11 o'clock while the first tennis match of the day _is_ (be) not until an hour later. The events _go on_ (go on) all day, so the boys _are not meeting_ (not meet) at the station again until the evening. Their train home _arrives_ (arrive) in Leicester at 10.15 pm.

8 Give help with *I'll* … (→ PB p. 11)

1. It's my job to *make* a poster for the judo competition, but I haven't got time.
   – I'm not so busy. _I'll make the poster._
2. Does anybody want to *go* to the football match with me? It isn't so much fun alone.
   – I enjoy football. _I'll go to the match with you._
3. Oh dear. I forgot to *get* the new 'Sidewalk' magazine when I was at the newsagent.
   – I'm going there later. _I'll get your magazine for you._
4. I want a cool photo of me on my skateboard – but I can't *take* my own photo!
   – Give me your camera. _I'll take a photo of you._
5. Would you like to *join* our new orienteering club? We haven't got many people yet.
   – Orienteering, you say? OK. _I'll join the club._

9 Make dialogues for the pictures (→ PB p. 11)

I'll …

Will you …?

Are the people asking for help or giving help? Write down their words in your exercise book. **(EH S. 86)**

TALKWISE

10 Use the right phrase for the situation (→ PB p. 12)

a) Which phrases are not polite? Underline them in red. Underline the polite phrases in blue.

That's rubbish! • Sorry, but I don't agree. • I see it differently. • Only an idiot could think that. • I'm not sure you're right. • You're so wrong. • Don't be silly! • I think the opposite is true.

b) *The second speakers in the dialogues want to show they do not agree. Do you think they are polite or not so polite? Choose phrases from a).* ***(Erwartungshorizont)***

1. United fan: United is the best team in the world!
   City fan: *That's rubbish!*
2. Reporter: Everyone thinks you'll lose.
   Tennis star: *I think the opposite is true.*
3. Shop assistant: This is the best bike for you.
   Customer: *I see it differently.*
4. Football referee: Your hand hit the ball.
   Angry player: *Only an idiot could think that.*

11 Make sentences with *I don't think …* (→ PB p. 12)

TIP

If you use the verb 'think' to explain a negative idea, it takes the 'not' from the other verb.
Example: He **doesn't train** hard enough. → I **don't think** he **trains** hard enough.

1. The referee wasn't fair to us. → I don't think the referee was *fair to us.*
2. He won't win the race. → I don't think he'll *win the race.*
3. She doesn't look very fit. → *I don't think she looks very fit.*
4. They didn't play very well. → *I don't think they played very well.*
5. I wouldn't like to play rugby. → *I don't think I'd like to play rugby.*

12 Your turn: Do you agree? (→ PB p. 12)

a) *Do you agree with these ideas or not? Use short answers to show what you think.*

1. "Skateboarding is a brilliant sport."
   You: *Yes, it is./No, it isn't.*
2. "Sports stars get too much money."
   You: *Yes, they do./No, they don't.*
3. "Most kids aren't fit enough."
   You: *Yes, they are./No, they aren't.*
4. "Germany has got a good football team."
   You: *Yes, it has./No, it hasn't.*
5. "A good tennis racket helps you to win."
   You: *Yes, it does./No, it doesn't.*
6. "Helmets don't look cool."
   You: *Yes, they do./No, they don't.*

b) *Work with a partner and compare your answers for a). Explain why you agreed or didn't agree.*

13 Draw a line through the relative pronouns which you cannot use (→ PB p. 14)

1. There are special TV channels for people (who • ~~which~~ • that • ~~whose~~) want to watch sports.
2. The money (~~who~~ • which • that • ~~whose~~) these channels make comes from commercial breaks.
3. There are lots of commercials (~~who~~ • which • that • ~~whose~~) use sports stars to sell things.
4. A fan (~~who~~ • ~~which~~ • ~~that~~ • whose) favourite star has something wants to have it, too.
5. Of course nobody (who • ~~which~~ • that • ~~whose~~) you see in a commercial does it for nothing.
6. So stars (~~who~~ • ~~which~~ • ~~that~~ • whose) success has already made them rich become even richer!

14 Practise sentences with relative clauses (→ PB p. 14)

a) *Tell your partner about things that you like, and also things that you don't like.*

Examples: I like games that you play with a ball.
I don't like people who only talk about sport.
I like kids whose hobbies are the same as mine.

I like I don't like	+	people • clothes • games stars • books • kids • …	+	who • whose that • which

b) *Now write down three things that your partner likes and three things that he / she doesn't like. Use your exercise book.* *(Erwartungshorizont S. 86)*

15 Write about a sports reporter's problems (→ PB p. 14)

TIP
Put the preposition at the end of the relative clause.

Use relative clauses to make one sentence from two.

1. He was interested in a swimmer. But the swimmer didn't want an interview.
   The swimmer who he was interested in didn't want an interview.
2. He hoped to talk to a football player. But the player wanted a lot of money.
   The football player who *he hoped to talk to wanted a lot of money.*
3. He waited for a top athlete. But the athlete forgot to meet him.
   The top athlete who he waited for forgot to meet him.
4. He expected to hear from a sports scientist. But she didn't answer his e-mail.
   The sports scientist who he expected to hear from didn't answer his e-mail.
5. He wanted information about a basketball star. But the star had no time.
   The basketball star who he wanted information about had no time.
6. He started an interview with a tennis player. But the player left to catch a plane.
   The tennis player who he started an interview with left to catch a plane.

16 Use contact clauses (→ PB p. 15)

Harry's class is doing a sports project with the title "You'll never believe it!" What does he tell his parents about the project? Finish the sentences with contact clauses.

TIP

It is normal to use contact clauses when you speak.

THINGS WE WANT TO FIND OUT FOR OUR PROJECT

1. What funny sports have people thought of?
2. What unusual records have athletes broken?
3. What silly mistakes have referees made?
4. What surprises have players had in events?
5. What crazy things have sports fans done?
6. What special skills have sports stars become famous for?

1. We're making a list of funny sports people have thought of.
2. We're collecting information about unusual records athletes have broken.
3. We're writing about silly mistakes referees have made.
4. We're describing surprises players have had in events.
5. We're finding out about crazy things sports fans have done.
6. We're giving examples of special skills sports stars have become famous for.

17 Listening: A ball kid at Wimbledon (→ PB p. 15) *(EH S. 86)*

a) *Listen to a ball kid and find information about these three words. Take notes in your exercise book.*

bird | racket | umpire

b) *Imagine you watched the match the ball kid is talking about. Write 6–8 sentences about the funny things that happened. The notes you took in a) will help you. Use your exercise book.*

18 Tandem activity: How to explain words you don't know (→ PB p. 15)

Decide who works with A and who works with B. You don't know the English words for the German words, so you must give definitions – in English, of course! (Relative clauses or the Useful phrases on page 15 in your book can help you.)

Take turns to explain your words and to guess your partner's words. When you guess correctly, write down the first letter of the German word in the box. Collect eight letters and make an English word that gives you the name of a sport.

A

Startschuss | Energie | Bewunderer | Lautsprecher | betrügen | atmen | loben | angreifen

Letters: MiWgmNSi

The sport is: swimming

B

messen | Sattel | gratulieren | Nationalhymne | imitieren | Mitglied | imponieren | Weitsprung

Letters: ESaBLbl

The sport is: baseball

19 An interview with a British champion (→ PB p. 18)

a) *Read the parts of an interview with Susan Jones from a magazine for young British readers. Don't worry about any new words. You will understand enough to match the answers to the questions. Put the correct numbers after the questions.*

Q: Hi, Susan. How old were you when you first started high jumping? A: 3

Q: What do you do to get ready before a big competition? A: 5

Q: What competitions have you won this season? A: 2

Q: What are your top tips for young high jumpers? A: 1

Q: What has been the most exciting moment in your career? A: 6

Q: How do you feel about the 2012 Olympic Games in London? A: 4

1. First, get into athletics and then try everything because you never know what you will be good at. Try to enjoy what you do for as long as you can. When training starts, it gets much harder.
2. I won the British championships, my fifth title in five years. I was hoping to go to the world championships, but I can't because I've got an injury.
3. I started athletics when I was 10 and got into high jumping when I was 11. There weren't enough girls in the high jump competition at my local club, so I competed and won a medal!
4. It's fantastic! I've always wanted to compete in the Olympic Games. So I'd really like to jump in the 2012 games and finish my athletics career there.
5. I always pack my bag the night before and make a list of things to do. I like to be organised. I'm also superstitious so I wear my lucky shoes for every competition.
6. There have been two. The first was when I won a silver medal at the Commonwealth Games, and the second was when I jumped my personal best of 1.95 m.

b) *Underline the new words in the interview. Find the words for these definitions.*

1. You get this when you hurt your body: injury
2. This describes something where you live: local
3. This is what you do when you are in a competition: compete
4. This is the time you spend in a job or in a sport: career
5. This describes someone who believes that special things bring good luck or bad luck: superstitious
6. This is your own record in your event: personal best

20 Writing texts: Write a story for the cartoon (→ PB p. 18) *(Erwartungshorizont S. 86)*

Look at the cartoon and write the story down in your exercise book. Use the past tense and write two or three sentences for every picture. Think of names for the boys.

You can start: Last Sunday … and … were having fun. They … But a neighbour …

VOCABULARY SKILLS

A B C D E F G H I

21 Put the German words into English (→ PB p. 19)

You already know two different English words for every German word.

1. schwer a) It's hard to do skateboard tricks. b) He's a big heavy player.
2. Geschichte a) The film tells a true story. b) Tennis has a long history.
3. tragen a) Please wear your helmet. b) I'll carry your bag for you.
4. Karte a) I need a new card for my camera. b) I've got a ticket for the big match.
5. ruhig a) You'll play better if you stay calm. b) Everyone was quiet – nobody spoke.

22 Use the context to find the correct word (→ PB p. 19)

Look at the different English words for 'Stoß'. Check the context of these words and match them with the pictures.

Stoß ❶ push, shove; [ʃʌv] **jemandem einen Stoß versetzen** give someone a push ❷ *(leichter Schlag)* nudge ❸ *(Erschütterung)* shock ❹ *(Stich)* stab ❺ *(Fechtstoß)* thrust ❻ *(Schwimmstoß)* stroke ❼ *(Haufen)* pile; *(größerer Haufen)* stack; *(Aktenstoß)* file [of deeds]; *(Papierstoß)* bundle

stroke nudge thrust pile push

1 thrust

2 push

3 stroke

4 pile

5 nudge

23 Mediation: Information on the Internet *(Lösungen S. 86)*

You and your friend find this home page on the Internet. Your friend cannot read English, so you must answer your friend's questions – in German, of course! Sometimes you must tell your friend that the answer is not on the page. With a partner, take turns to ask and answer the questions.

ARE YOU ADVENTUROUS AND DARING? ARE YOU LOOKING FOR A NEW HOBBY WHERE YOU CAN MEET LOTS OF COOL PEOPLE AND GET AN ADRENALINE RUSH AS WELL? THEN OUR SKATEBOARDING CLUB IS MOST DEFINITELY FOR YOU! WE HAVE GOT SOMETHING FOR EVERYBODY, THE GIRLS AND THE GUYS. IF YOU WANT TO LEARN HOW TO BE A REAL SKATEBOARDER AND DO TRICKS LIKE AN INDY AND A NOSEGRIND, THEN HURRY UP AND JOIN OUR CLUB!!! AND REMEMBER SKATEBOARDING ISN'T JUST A HOBBY; IT IS A WAY TO GET AROUND AND ALSO AN ART FORM.

What we offer:

- different learning groups, depending on your skateboarding experience
- trick workshops where you can learn the most radical tricks
- safety instructions so you don't break an arm when you perform that Indy
- access to our awesome skatepark, with everything you need to have a killer time
- your personal membership card, which allows you to get special prices at certain skateboarding stores

SKATEBOARDING CLUB

1. Hat der Klub seinen eigenen Skatepark?
2. Kann man in dem Club auch als Anfänger / -in Mitglied werden?
3. Was kostet es, Mitglied zu werden?
4. Welche Vorteile bringt der Mitgliedsausweis?
5. Gibt es auch Sicherheitstraining?
6. Was meinen sie mit dem Satz über Skateboardfahren als Hobby?

24 Make pairs of words with almost the same meaning (→ PB p. 20)

skill | train ✔ | fast | pitch | hope | fans | players | field | quick | practise ✔ | team | trick | champion | home crowd | competition | event | chance | winner ✔

1. train — practise
2. winner — champion
3. fans – home crowd
4. pitch – field
5. fast – quick
6. team – players
7. hope – chance
8. competition – event
9. trick – skill

25 Find words that go together (→ PB p. 20)

Write down a partner word from the box.
Then explain what links the two words. (EH)

track | swim | oval | hand | control | celebrate | bat ✔

1. cricket – bat: In cricket you hit the ball with a bat.
2. win – celebrate: You celebrate when you win because you are happy.
3. rugby – oval: You play rugby with an oval ball.
4. run – track: In athletics you run on a track.
5. referee – control: The referee controls the game.
6. wave – hand: You use your hand when you wave to someone.
7. goggles – swim: If you wear goggles when you swim, water doesn't get in your eyes.

26 Put in the prepositions the football fans use (→ PB p. 20)

1. Wow! He's the best player on the pitch! 2. Come on! We're waiting for a goal! 3. Our team is better than yours! 4. Why didn't the idiot give the ball to somebody else? 5. This is the best game of the season so far! 6. Ha ha! Look what has happened to the referee!

27 Collect verbs (Erwartungshorizont)

Write down as many examples as you can of …

1. what fans do at sports events.
   shout, clap, wave, jump, cry, sing, laugh, …
2. what you can do with a ball.
   hold, kick, hit, catch, throw, carry, lose, …

28 Say what you are doing at the weekend (→ PB p. 21) *(Lösungsvorschlag)*

Charlie invited Frank over to his house, but Frank doesn't want to visit him.
He tells Charlie that he has got other arrangements. Complete Frank's answers with your own ideas.
Use the present progressive.

Charlie: Would you like to come over to my house on Saturday morning?

Frank: Thanks, but *I'm helping my mother with the shopping* on Saturday morning.

Charlie: Oh, I see. Have you got time in the afternoon?

Frank: No, sorry. *I'm watching a skateboard competition* on Saturday afternoon.

Charlie: Well, how about Sunday morning? Can you come over then?

Frank: No, I can't. *I'm going swimming* on Sunday morning.

Charlie: Hm. I expect you've got other arrangements for Sunday afternoon, too. Right?

Frank: Yes, *I'm visiting my grandma* on Sunday afternoon.

29 Put in the correct relative pronouns (→ PB p. 21)

a) *Use:* who • whose • which

1. Eddie the Eagle is the ski jumper *who* became famous at the 1988 Winter Olympics. 2. He didn't look like the other stars *who* the fans came to watch. 3. He wore glasses *which* misted up under his goggles. 4. There was nobody *whose* jumps were like Eddie's. 5. The jumps *which* he did were only good enough for last place. 6. But Eddie was more popular than the man *who* won the gold medal. 7. Everyone enjoyed the stories *which* he told about his adventures. 8. And it was Eddie *whose* friendly face everyone wanted to see.

b) You can also use the relative pronoun 'that' in sentences: *1* – *2* – *3* – *5* – *6* – *7*

c) You can make a contact clause without a relative pronoun in sentences: *2* – *5* – *7*

30 Complete the dialogue with Useful phrases from page 12 in your book (→ PB p. 21)

A: Sports stars should be friendly to the people who go and watch them.

B: *I agree.* Their fans are an important part of their success.

A: *Exactly!* I mean, without fans nobody is a star!

B: *You're right.* But most big sports stars are nice and friendly.

A: *I don't think that's true.* A lot of them aren't interested in their fans.

B: *I don't agree.* Maybe there are one or two stars like that, but not many.

⟨Point Blank[1]⟩

Alex Rider is fourteen when he gets drawn into the British Secret service, MI 6. Like a teenage James Bond, Alex starts to solve difficult cases for them. In Point Blank, he is sent to an elite school for rebellious kids. Alex finds himself stuck in a boarding school high atop the Swiss Alps with the sons of the rich and powerful. Read how Alex manages to escape from his prison …

He waited until the guard[2] had gone, then stole into the laundry room[3] a few doors down. When he came out, he was carrying a long, flat object made of lightweight aluminium. He carried it into his bedroom, closed the door, and turned on one small lamp. He was afraid the guard would see the light if he returned. But he couldn't work in the dark. It was a risk he had to take.

He had stolen an ironing board[4]. […]

Carefully, he took up his position on the ironing board, his right foot at forty degrees, his left foot at twenty. He was goofy-footed[5]. That was what the snowboarding instructor had told him. His feet should have been the other way around. But this was no time to worry about technique. Instead, he used the strips of torn[6] sheet[7] to tie the ironing board to his feet, then he stood where he was, contemplating[8] what he was about to do. He had only travelled down green and blue runs - the colours given to the beginners' and intermediate slopes. He knew from James that this mountain was an expert black all the way down. Could he do it? Could he trust himself?

An alarm bell exploded behind him. Lights came on throughout the academy. Alex pushed forward and set off, picking up speed with every second. The decision had been made for him. Now, whatever happened, there could be no going back.

Dr Grief, wearing a long silver dressing gown, stood beside the open window in Alex's room.

[…] "He must be walking down the mountain-side," Mrs Stellenbosch said. "he has no skis. He won't make it. We can wait until morning and pick him up in the helicopter."

"I think the boy may be more inventive[9] than we believe." Dr Grief picked up the remains[10] of the ironing board. "You see? He has improvised some sort of sledge. All right …" He had come to a decision. Mrs Stellenbosch was glad to see the certainty[11] return to his eyes. "I want two men on snowmobiles, following him down. Now!" One of the guards hurried out of the room. "What about the unit at the foot of the mountain?" Mrs Stellenbosch said.

"Indeed." Dr Grief smiled. He had always kept a man and a driver at the end of the last valley in case anybody ever tried to leave the academy on skis. […] "Whatever he's using, he'll be unable to cross the railway line. We can have a machine gun set up, waiting for him. Assuming[12] he does manage to get that far, he'll be a sitting duck[13]."

"Excellent," Mrs Stellenbosch purred. […]

Alex had been travelling for several minutes and so far he had fallen only twice – both times into thick banks of snow that had protected[14] him. How far down could it be?

And then he heard the sound coming up behind him. […] Alex leapt forward, diving into the next slope. At the same time, there was a series of distant cracks, and the snow flew up all around him. Grief's men had machine guns built into their snowmobiles! Alex yelled as he swooped down the mountainside, barely able to control the sheet of metal under his feet. […]

The two men in the gray van saw Alex snowboarding toward them. They were parked on a road on the other side of the railway line and had been waiting only a few minutes. […] Every second brought him closer to them. There was nowhere for him to hide.

And then there was a sudden blast as a train exploded out of the tunnel. It was a freight train, travelling about twenty miles an hour. It had at least thirty train cars being pulled by a diesel engine, and it formed a moving wall between Alex and the gun, protecting him. But it would be there only a few seconds. He had to move fast.

adapted from: *Point Blank. An Alex Rider Adventure* by Anthony Horowitz

[1] **point blank** (ˌpɔɪnt ˈblæŋk) = Kernschuss • [2] **guard** (gɑ:d) = Wärter • [3] **laundry room** (ˈlɔ:ndri ˌrʊm) = Waschküche • [4] **ironing board** (ˈaɪənɪŋ ˌbɔ:d) = Bügelbrett • [5] **goofy-footed** (ˈgu:fi ˌfʊtɪd) = *beim Skateboarden: rechtes Bein vorne, linkes Bein hinten* • [6] **torn** (tɔ:n) = zerrissen • [7] **sheet** (ʃi:t) = Laken • [8] **(to) contemplate** (ˈkɒntəmpleɪt) = nachdenken • [9] **inventive** (ɪnˈventɪv) = erfinderisch, einfallsreich • [10] **remains** (rɪˈmeɪnz) = Überbleibsel • [11] **certainty** (ˈsə:tnti) = Gewissheit • [12] **(to) assume** (əˈsju:m) = annehmen • [13] **sitting duck** (ˌsɪtɪŋ ˈdʌk) = leichte Beute • [14] **(to) protect** (prəˈtekt) = schützen

Unit 2 Once upon a time …

1 Different ages in history (→ PB p. 24)

a) *Read what Historia says and put the texts in the right time order (numbers 1–7).*

4 I work on an English ship, and I enjoy the trips to America. But today I'm scared! They say 130 ships from another country are going to attack us! I hope our captain has got a good plan … **T**

7 Our country has joined a big new club. Germany, France, Italy and lots of other countries are in it, too. But not Canada. – That's too far away. **Y**

2 It's a very sad time for us in England. Our king died in a battle yesterday, and many of our soldiers are dead, too. Now we have a new king from another country. **I**

5 I've made a great invention! It's a new kind of power, and it's so easy. – You just need a really hot fire and some water … **O**

Hi! I'm Historia again. Can you find out where I am?

1 It's so cold and wet here, – very different from my home! I'm building a long, straight road. People will still use it thousands of years from now. Now I – Oh no! Here's the caretaker! Goodbye! **H**

6 I work on a ship which travels all round the world. We buy things cheaply in our colonies, then we take them to our factories at home. Somebody must become very rich – but it isn't me! **R**

3 Life is very hard for poor people like me. I must work all day on Sir Percy's farm. It's terrible. – And I can't understand the language these knights speak! **S**

b) *Write the letters from the texts in the right order. – You have learnt a lot about this.*

H	I	S	T	O	R	Y

c) *Write one sentence about each of the seven ages in a) in your exercise book. (Don't forget to use the past tense.)* **(Erwartungshorizont S. 86)**

Example: 1. The Romans also built walls and buildings in England.

2 Listening: When is it? (→ PB p. 25)

Listen to the people again and cross out the wrong words or phrases.

1. One woman is crying because Harold • ~~is in India~~ • must go to India • ~~has not come home yet~~.
2. The woman is worried about • ~~the large army~~ • ~~the Indian weather~~ • the wild animals.
3. One of the boys is going to work • ~~on a farm~~ • ~~in a shop in Manchester~~ • in a shoe factory.
4. People on farms work • ~~ten hours a day~~ • twelve hours a day • ~~ten hours on Saturdays~~.

3 Revision: Modals (→ PB p. 27)

Some pupils are talking to their teacher about their trip to the theatre next week. Finish the sentences with modals.

TIP
You know these modals:
may / can / can't
must / mustn't / needn't

1. "*May* I use my mobile in the theatre?" – "Oh no, you *mustn't / can't* do that!"
2. "I *can't* buy any cool new clothes for the theatre. They cost too much." – "Don't worry. You *needn't* wear expensive clothes."
3. "Sorry, I *can't* come to the theatre on Friday." – "You *must* come! I've bought you a ticket!"
4. "*Must* we read the play before we see it?" – "No, you *needn't* do that, but you *can* check the Internet for information, if you like."

4 *Können* or *dürfen*? (→ PB p. 27)

a) *Read the sentences. Underline* **can / can't** *= 'können' in one colour,* **can / can't** *= 'dürfen' in another.*

1. Matt can't take photos in the theatre.
2. Sue can't understand Russian.
3. Every pupil can borrow two books from the library.
4. Jack can't go to the concert without a ticket.
5. Amy can swim 50 metres under water.

b) *Rewrite the sentences in your exercise book with* **is / isn't able to** *or* **is / isn't allowed to**. (Lösungen S. 86)

5 What can Alex do? (→ PB p. 27)

a) *What will he be able to do in the future?*

1. When he's older, *he'll be able to play the guitar.*
2. In three years from now *he'll be able to speak Spanish.*
3. If he practises hard, *he'll be able to jump two metres.*

b) *What about when Alex was a little boy? What does he remember?*

Internet alone
TV
holiday – friends

1. "When I was only seven, *I wasn't allowed to use the Internet alone.*
2. *But I was allowed to watch TV.*
3. *I wasn't allowed to go on holiday with my friends*."

6 Francis Drake's house (→ PB p. 28)

*Choose the correct form of **able to** or **allowed to**.*

TIP
able to – können
allowed to – dürfen

wasn't allowed to | was able to … | wasn't able to … | were allowed to … ✔ | weren't allowed to … | will be able to …

Last year Tracy and her friends were allowed to go to Devon for a holiday. They visited Buckland Abbey[1], Francis Drake's house, but they weren't allowed to look at all the rooms. Drake wasn't able to spend a lot of time there because he was often at sea. Tracy wanted to try on some of the clothes, but she wasn't allowed to do that. But she was able to buy postcards of the dresses. When she goes to London next month, she will be able to take photos of Drake's ship on the Thames.

7 *Have to* (→ PB p. 28)

Tina, a visitor from Canada, is very interested in English history. She is talking to a guide in a famous house where Queen Elizabeth I lived as a girl.
*Complete the text with forms of **have to** (past tense, will future).*

Tina: Did Elizabeth have to go to school while she lived here? *(Elizabeth • go)*

Guide: No, she didn't have to go anywhere. Her teachers came to her! *(she • not • go)*

Tina: Did all girls have lessons in those days?

Guide: No, – many people thought girls didn't have to learn much. Elizabeth was lucky – and clever, too. *(girls • not • learn)*

Tina: Did she live here until she became Queen?

Guide: No, she had other homes. And she had to live in the Tower of London as a prisoner for two months! *(she • live)*

Tina: Wow! Did she try to run away?

Guide: I'm not sure about that, sorry. You'll have to ask your History teacher. *(you • ask)*

Tina: OK, I will. Did Elizabeth come back here when she was Queen?

Guide: Not very often. She visited many other houses, and the hosts had to pay for their expensive guest! *(the hosts • pay)*

[1] **Buckland Abbey** [ˌbʌklənd 'æbi] in Yelverton ['jelvətn], Devon ['devn]

8 Tandem activity: A visit to the cinema (→ PB p. 28)

Jenny is asking her friend Mark about his class trip to London last week. Decide who is A and who is B. (Jenny asks the questions, and Mark answers them.) Watch out for signal words for the tenses! When you have finished the dialogue once, change roles.
▲ = 'able to'; ◆ = 'allowed to' ■ = 'have to'. Check your partner's sentences.

A Jenny

1. you – ■ – visit museums – every day – on trip?
(No, yesterday we were allowed to see "the Armada" at the Odeon.)
2. you – ■ – queue – cinema?
(No, we didn't. We were able to buy tickets earlier.)
3. you – ▲ – read – book – "Drake's Armada" – yet?
(No, I haven't. I'll be allowed to borrow it from my brother next week.)
4. How – English – ▲ – defeat – Spanish Armada?
(There were many reasons. Maybe the Spanish were not able to sail in bad English weather.)
5. you – ■ – write – report – trip – next week?
(Yes, I will. But I'm allowed to / I'll be allowed to write it with my friends.)

B Mark

1. (Did you have to visit museums every day on your trip?)
No – yesterday – we – ◆ – see "The Armada" – Odeon
2. (Did you have to queue at the cinema?)
No – we – ▲ – buy tickets – earlier
3. (Have you been able to read the book "Drake's Armada" yet?)
No – I – ◆ borrow – my brother – next week
4. (How were the English able to defeat the Spanish Armada?)
many reasons – maybe – Spanish – not – ▲ – sail – bad English weather
5. (Will you have to write a report about your trip next week?)
Yes – but – I – ◆ – write – with friends

9 A game: Ask clever questions (→ PB p. 28)

Play this game in two teams, A and B. One or two players are not in a team. – They are referees.

a) *Before you start to play, make 12 cards. Write 'able to' on four of them, 'allowed to' on another four, and 'have to' on the rest. Mix them well!*

b) *A player in team A reads one sentence from this list to a pupil in team B:*
Queen Victoria often went on holiday to Scotland.
My brothers are going to build a steam engine next week.
Jane wants to visit the British Museum on Monday.
The Saxons lost their land when the Normans came.
In the 18th century many families went to live in the cities.
A new wax museum will open on 10th December.
Roman soldiers often walked along Hadrian's Wall.
Ed Jones is planning a new film about Queen Elizabeth I.

c) *The player in team B takes the first card and looks at it. He / She must ask the pupil in team A a question with the verb on the card. (Be careful of the tense!) If the question is good, team B gets a point. (The referees can give an extra point for a funny question.) Then a player from team B reads a sentence from the list in b). After that two different players are the referees.*

10 Mediation: How to – Visit a museum (→ PB p. 28)

a) *You want to visit a museum in an English city. At the ticket office a German woman and her three children ask for your help.*

VICTORIA MUSEUM

Admission

Adults	£8.00
Children 4–16 (under 4: free)	£4.00
Full-time students	£4.00
Family ticket (up to 2 adults, up to 3 children under 16)	£15.00

Woman: Entschuldige, bitte – dort steht etwas von „family“. Gibt es einen Sonderpreis für uns?

You: Ja. – Wenn Ihre Kinder unter ***16 sind, kostet es £15.00.***

Boy: Ich bin erst 10. Haben sie alte Maschinen hier?

You: Ich weiß nicht. Ich frag' mal die Führerin hier.

Excuse me, ***are there any old machines in the museum?***

Guide: Yes, there are steam engines and other machines on the second floor.

You: ***Es gibt Dampfmaschinen und andere Maschinen im zweiten Stock.***

Boy: Darf man damit spielen?

You: ***Are we allowed to play with them?***

Guide: No, you aren't, sorry. But there's a short film about the machine that you can watch.

You: ***Nein. Aber es gibt einen kurzen Film, den man sich anschauen kann.***

Woman: Darf ich diese Tasche mit ins Museum nehmen?

You: ***Can she take that bag into the museum?***

Guide: No, it's too big. She can leave it in one of the lockers over there.

You: ***Nein, die Tasche ist zu groß. Sie können sie in einem der Schließfächer dort drüben lassen.***

Boy: Und mein Fotoapparat? Muss ich den auch hier lassen?

You: ***What about the boy's camera? Must he leave it here, too?***

Guide: No, he can take it with him. But please don't take any photos inside the museum. We have a large museum shop with postcards, books, DVDs …

You: ***Du kannst den Fotoapparat mitnehmen, aber du darfst im Museum nicht fotografieren. Es gibt einen großen Laden mit Postkarten, Büchern, DVDs …***

Boy: Super. Ich gehe zuerst dorthin! Vielen Dank!

b) *What kind of museum would you like to visit? A museum for clothes? Technology? History? Think of five questions which you would like to ask a guide at your museum.*
Use the Useful phrases on p. 28 in your book. Write the questions in your exercise book. ***(Erwartungshorizont S. 86)***

TALKWISE

11 Listening: A class trip to Stratford (→ PB p. 29)

Last month Class 9JF read a play by Shakespeare. Now they are planning a trip to Shakespeare's town, Stratford-upon-Avon[1].

a) *Listen to the CD. Fill in the information about the pupils' plans. (Notes only.)*

Subject	What they could do	What they decide to do
Transport	bus, train, car	bus
Food	restaurant, snack bar, picnic (sandwiches)	picnic
Sights and activities	Shakespeare's house, Visitor Centre, theatre, boat trip / picnic	Shakespeare's house, Visitor Centre, boat trip / picnic

b) *Making suggestions: Listen again. Which of these Useful phrases did you hear?*

I've got an idea.	☐	I suggest …	☑	I think we ought to …	☑
We could …	☑	How about …	☑	Shouldn't we …	☐

c) *Write down two more Useful phrases which you heard.*

Why don't we / you … ? Shall I … ? We can …

12 Your turn: Plan a party (→ PB p. 29) *(Erwartungshorizont)*

a) *You want to organise a party together with a partner. Make notes.*

When?	next Saturday evening
Where?	at our house
Who? (invitations)	all our friends in our class; friends from the sports club
Food?	pizza, salads, crisps, ice-cream
Music?	my CD player; ask everyone to bring favourite CDs
… ?	parents, suggest cinema

b) *Talk about your ideas with your partner. (Look at his / her notes, too.) Decide which suggestions are best, then make a plan: Who is going to do what? Use the Useful phrases on p. 29 in your book.*

[1] **Stratford-upon-Avon** [ˌstrætfəd əpɒnˈeɪvn]

13 The past perfect (→ PB p. 31)

Look at the pictures and write about Leo's visit to Warwick[1] Castle.

1. After Leo had read a book about castles, he visited Warwick Castle.
2. As soon as he had entered the hall, his mobile rang.
3. When he had climbed the tower, he had a wonderful view.
4. After he had bought some postcards, he had a drink in the cafeteria.

14 A famous Victorian: Simple past or past perfect? (→ PB p. 31)

Isambard Kingdom Brunel[2] (1806–1859) was one of the most famous English engineers[3] of the 19th century. He went (go) to school in France, and as soon as he had finished (finish) his education there, he began (begin) to work with his father on a tunnel under the Thames in London. They finished (finish) the tunnel in 1841, although a bad accident had almost killed (almost kill) Isambard in 1828. When the new East London Railway[4] started (start) in 1869, it was (be) able to use the Thames Tunnel which the Brunels had built (build). In the 18th century people had begun (begin) to use iron[5] for bridges, and later Isambard Brunel built (build) some of the longest bridges in the world. He made (make) very large ships of iron, too. They worked (work) with steam engines, which James Watt had invented (invent) more than 50 years before. Brunel's biggest ship was the "Great Eastern". When Brunel died (die) in 1859, it had not yet started (not yet start) on its first trip to New York, but it crossed (cross) the ocean to America many times between 1859 and 1867.

[1] **Warwick** ['wɒrɪk] • [2] **Isambard Kingdom Brunel** [ˌɪzmbɑːd ˌkɪŋdəm 'bruːnel] • [3] **engineer** [ˌendʒɪ'nɪə] = Ingenieur •
[4] **railway** ['reɪlweɪ] = Eisenbahn • [5] **iron** [aɪən] = Eisen

READING SKILLS

15 A historical story (→ PB p. 32)

A Pre-reading

Talk to your partner about the title and the picture.
Discuss what you already know about this age and write down notes together.

B First Reading *(Erwartungshorizont S. 86)*

Read the text quickly, then answer these questions in 1–3 words each (write the answers in your exercise book):

WHO? WHEN? WHERE? WHAT?

The story of a hard life

Hannah Todd worked in the Lonsdale Factory near Manchester for more than thirteen years. Her name is there on the factory lists.

Her family came from London, and she had three brothers. Her father died when she was six. Soon her mother had no money left, and she did not know how she could feed her hungry children. There was only one kind of place for poor people like the Todds – the workhouse[1]. They did not have to pay any money there, but everybody had to work very hard. The meals were bad, so the people were often hungry. There were very strict rules, too. Children were not allowed to be with their parents very often, and the girls were not together with the boys. Hannah was very lonely without her family.

Soon after her tenth birthday a man came to the workhouse and told Hannah about a new job for her in the north of England. Hannah was very scared, but her mother told her, "It's better for you this way. You'll have good food and clothes, and you'll learn to read and write." That was in 1837, the year Victoria became Queen.

Hannah lived with about a hundred poor children in a big house near the Lonsdale Factory. The owner needed more workers, and children were cheap, even if he had to feed them. The house was Hannah's home for the next eight years – years of hard work in the factory, twelve

hours a day. The machines were loud and scary. Hannah soon learnt how to be quick and not to fall asleep, so she never had a bad accident. In some ways her mother had been right. Here she always had three meals a day, sometimes with vegetables from the garden. She had some school lessons after work – and a doctor came when a child was really ill. She didn't earn any money, but it was much better than the workhouse.

When Hannah was 18, she left the house and got a better job at the factory. Five years later she stopped working there – her name is no longer on the lists. Maybe she was married and looked after her family. Or she became ill and was not able to work. A church list tells us that she died in 1870 – the year that the government opened free schools for all children.

C Second Reading

a) *Read each part of the text slowly. Mark important information. Mark words you may want to look up later.*

b) *Make an action line for Hannah in your exercise book.*
(Erwartungshorizont S. 86)

D A closer look

a) *What have you learnt about Hannah's character? Write about her in your exercise book.* *(Erwartungshorizont S. 86)*

b) *Find out more about Victorian children like Hannah. Use libraries and the Internet.*

[1] **workhouse** ['wɜːkhaʊs] = Armenhaus

16 Who says what? (→ PB p. 35)

a) *Look at the story on pages 33–35 in your book. Which sentence goes where? Look at the pictures and write the words in the correct speech bubble.*

The Robinsons? They've gone away. | Welcome to our house, Gwendolyn. | Help, help! Pull me out!

We can't help them anyway. | … servant has sixth sense …

These names are so funny! | I'm sorry. Please try to understand. | She's scared for her daughter.

b) *Put the pictures from the story of Chloe and Alex in the right order. Put the numbers 1–? in the box.*

c) *Now do the same with the pictures from the story of Gwendolyn and Timothy. (a–?)*

17 Writing texts: Write a diary (→ PB p. 35) *(Erwartungshorizont S. 86)*

Imagine Chloe's mother kept a diary, too. What did she write down on days that are important for our story?

Example: 10 June 2006: Today I found my great-grandmother's diary. …
15 March 2007: I went to the town library to check …

18 The odd one out

Which word is wrong? Underline it. Look at the wrong word again and then at the other words. Can you think of a word family for the wrong word and the other words? Write them in the grid.

	Word family	
	for the wrong word	**for the other words**
1. oil – wood – stage – metal	theatre	raw materials
2. empress – throne – heir – servant	thing	people
3. to laugh – to gasp – to attack – to cry	activity	voice / sound
4. prison – factory – fortress – tribe	people	places
5. sad – excited – angry – lonely	positive feeling	negative feeling

19 Listening: Sounds – Sentence stress (→ PB p. 36)

a) *Listen to the sentence. Which of the "important words" are the most important? Underline them.*

The **story** which **Gwendolyn** heard from **Timothy** was so **scary** that she wasn't **able** to **sleep** that **night**.

b) *Underline the important words in these sentences and read them aloud. Remember to stress the important words. Then compare your ideas with the CD.*

1. If you go to see a play by Shakespeare, you may find his language difficult to understand.
2. How about a visit to the Tower if the weather is too stormy for a boat trip?

Which of the words you have underlined are the most important? Put a circle round them.

20 Word pairs that sound the same

Read the word pairs on the right. Use the word pairs to finish the sentences.

heir / air
steal / steel
rain / reign
knew / new
week / weak
night / knight
would / wood

1. Did it rain on the first day of Queen Victoria's reign?
2. Everyone knew about Watt's new invention.
3. Somebody tried to steal Lady Cumberland's new steel pen.
4. One night, a Norman knight lost his horse in the dark.
5. The men would like to build with wood, not metal.
6. When the king died, his heir was outside in the fresh air.
7. After just one week everyone knew Elizabeth was not a weak queen.

21 Have to, able to or allowed to (→ PB p. 37)

Use the correct tenses. Watch out for signal words.

Film star Jake Harding often acts in historical films.

"Last year I played Francis Drake. We *had to* work in terrible weather, but nobody *was allowed to* wear an anorak, of course! Next April everybody *will be able to* see the film at the cinema. My worst moment as Francis Drake? I fell into the sea in Mexico, but luckily I *was able to* swim to the beach. I've just started on a new film – I'm Queen Victoria's son. We hope we *will be allowed to* film in Buckingham Palace." Jake's fans *won't have to* (not) wait long to see him. His film "Empire" is on TV tomorrow evening.

22 Finish the dialogues (→ PB p. 37) *(Lösungsvorschlag)*

What can you say? Use the Useful phrases on page 29 in your book .

1. What can we do this weekend? – *How about a trip to the castle?*
2. It's a long way to walk, but the bus is so expensive! – *I suggest we go by bike.*
3. I'm sure we can buy a snack when we get there. – *Shouldn't we take sandwiches?*
4. I'd like to find out about the place before we go. – *Why don't you check the Internet?*

23 Busy servant's day (→ PB p. 37)

What did Molly do in Lady Dunmore's house yesterday?

Molly got up at 5.30.

1. After *she had made breakfast, she worked in the kitchen.*
2. As soon as *she had cleaned the living room, she went to the market.*
3. When *she had cooked lunch, she washed up.*
4. After *she had cleaned the kitchen, she mended some clothes.*
5. As soon as *she had prepared the vegetables, she cooked dinner.*
6. After *she had written a letter to her parents, she went to bed at 9.30.*

⟨Revision for tests⟩ Unit 1–2

1 At Epic Skatepark

Put in a verb or a modal auxiliary. Watch out for the right tense and form!

Laura *was training* (train) at Epic Skatepark in Birmingham. Some of the other skaters *wanted* (want) to make a video of her new trick, but they *weren't allowed to do* (can • not • do) that. The big event was only a few days away. She *had to be* (must • be) careful, because she *didn't want* (not • want) anyone to steal her surprise. She *wasn't/hadn't been able to do* (can • not • do) the trick at first. After she *had practised* (practise) really hard for three weeks the trick *was* (be) perfect. She *didn't have to think* (need • not • think) about what she *had to do* (must • do) – she just did it. As soon as she *had finished* (finish) training she *went* (go) to the changing room. Harry met her outside. "I'm sure you *will be able to win* (can • win) the competition with that trick," he said. "You *will have to call* (must • call) it the 'Laura Spin' after you *have won* (win) and are Champion of the World! – well, of Birmingham …

2 Write a letter to the school magazine *(Erwartungshorizont S. 87)*

In last month's school magazine, a pupil wrote an article about P.E. at the school. The pupils want new sports like skateboarding, in-line skating, orienteering, climbing or golf in P.E. lessons.

Do you think this is a good idea or not? Make notes in two lists. Then write a letter to the magazine. The Useful phrases on page 12 in your book can help you.

3 Plan a sports evening with your parents

Your P. E. teacher wants to have a sports evening with pupils and their parents in the school sports hall. He has asked the class to think about it. Talk about your plans with your partner. Use the Useful phrases on page 29 in your book.

Example:

You: How about asking our brothers and sisters to come, too?
Your partner: Good idea! We could play …

4 Trafalgar, 1805 *(EH S. 87)*

a) ***Pre-reading:***
1. *What do you think of when you hear the word 'Trafalgar'?*
2. *Look at the title and at the picture painted by William Turner[1]. Say what you think the text is about.*

b) ***Reading for the gist:*** *Read the text quickly and answer these questions.*
- *What is the text about?*
- *When does it happen?*
- *Where does it happen?*
- *What happens?*

The Battle of Trafalgar, as seen from the Victory (William Turner, 1806–1808)

It was early morning, at about 8 am, when one of the French ships first saw the British ships in the west. After they had sent a signal to Admiral Villeneuve[2] he tried to get the French and Spanish ships into a line, but it was not easy, because the big ships could not turn quickly.

On the *Victory*[3] Nelson told one of his lieutenants[4], Pasco, to send a signal to all the British ships: "England expects every man to do his duty." Some time after 10 am the Battle of Trafalgar, which is one of the most famous sea battles in English history, started. It was 21st October 1805 near Cape[5] Trafalgar on the Spanish coast.

As *Victory* got nearer to the French and Spanish line the enemy killed and hurt a lot of the men badly. Nelson had his medals[6] on his uniform, so it was easy to see who he was. Soon *Victory* was very close to one of the French ships, and they crashed together. The noise was terrible – mens' shouts, men in great pain. At about 1.15 pm there was a shot from the French ship which hit the top of Nelson's shoulder. It was Nelson's last sea battle. He knew he was going to die. Maybe he knew he was going to die in this battle. He had written 'goodbye letters' to Lady Hamiliton[7], who was not his wife, and to their daughter Horatia[8], and he had asked friends to look after them after he had died.

Fighting continued into the afternoon. Ships lost their sails and were not able to sail on the high waves. Clouds of smoke hid the enemy ships, but the British were winning the battle. One by one the French and Spanish ships sailed away. Captain Hardy[9] reported to Nelson that they had defeated the enemy. "Thank God I have done my duty" were his last words, and he died at 4.30 pm.

The next time you are in London, go to Trafalgar Square. You will be able to see Lord Horatio[10] Nelson at the top of the column[11] – Nelson's Column.

c) ***Reading for detail:***
1. *Who are the important people in the text?*
2. *Make a time line for what happened.*

d) ***Writing texts:*** *Choose one of these ideas.*
1. *Captain Hardy writes a letter to Lady Hamiliton and / or Horatia after the battle. Captain Hardy does not know Lady Hamilton or her daughter, but was with Nelson at sea for a long time.*
2. *You are standing on the Victory. Look at the picture and think of what you can see, hear and smell. Make a word web with your ideas before you start to write.*

[1] **Turner** ['tɜ:nə] • [2] **Admiral Villeneuve** [ˌædmrəl 'vi:lnɜ:v] • [3] **Victory** ['vɪktri] • [4] **lieutenant** [lef'tenənt] = Leutnant • [5] **Cape** [keɪp] = Kap • [6] **medal** ['medl] = Medaille • [7] **Hamilton** ['hæmltən] • [8] **Horatia** [hə'reɪʃə] • [9] **Hardy** [hɑ:di] • [10] **Horatio** [hə'reɪʃiəʊ] • [11] **column** ['kɒləm]= Säule

Unit 3 Living together

1 Write down what you think the people are saying (→ PB p. 43) *(Erwartungshorizont)*

1. A: *Your music is driving me crazy!*
   B: *If you don't like it, go somewhere else!*
2. A: *Hurry up! I want to use the bathroom.*
   B: *Boys want to look good, too, you know!*
3. A: *Please! I really need my pocket money now.*
   B: *I don't care. You must wait until Saturday.*

2 Mobile text English (→ PB p. 43)

a) *Write this text message in normal English.*

```
Miriam, Y don't U want
2 C me? Please B my
girlfriend agN. U R the
only 1 4 me! I will call
L8er + talk 2 U. Jake
```

Miriam, why don't you want to see me?
Please be my girlfriend again. You are the only
one for me! I will call later and talk to you. Jake

b) *Write your own short text message to a friend. Use your exercise book.* *(EH S. 87)*

3 Your turn: Family life (→ PB p. 43) *(EH S. 87)*

Write sentences about your family in your exercise book.

Example: It drives me crazy when my parents ask me lots of questions about school.

It drives me crazy when …
I'm glad that …
I really like it when …
I sometimes get fed up because …
It's so embarrassing when …

4 Listening: A telephone message (→ PB p. 43)

Compare the dialogue with the message on the answerphone. Underline the mistakes, then write the dialogue again with the correct words. Use your exercise book.

Cleaning lady: Hello, Mr Patterson. What are you doing this morning?
Grandpa Patterson: Oh, I'm just sitting in front of the window.
Cleaning lady: That's nice. But this room is dirty, isn't it? Hm, what have you eaten today?
Grandpa Patterson: Just breakfast. I haven't been to the shops, you see.
Cleaning lady: I'm going to make you a nice sandwich. Then I'm going to go shopping with you.

5 What are the parents and kids saying? (→ PB p. 45)

a) *Put in the correct reflexive forms.*

myself | yourself✓ | himself | herself | itself | ourselves | yourselves | themselves

1. "I think you should prepare yourself for a shock. Look!" 2. "It's time for its food. It isn't able to feed itself, you know." 3. "Don't worry! We're old enough to look after ourselves." 4. "What a horrible sound! Can't he hear himself?" 5. "Parents sometimes need to have a good time and enjoy themselves, too." 6. "How often do I have to repeat myself before you understand?' 7. "Stop that, you two! Sit down and behave yourselves." 8. "Oh, dear. That doesn't look safe. If she isn't careful, she'll hurt herself."

b) *Talk with your partner about the sentences in a). Who do you think is speaking: a parent or a kid? What could the scene be?*

6 Put the German verbs into English (→ PB p. 45)

A German girl is writing to an English friend. Are the verbs reflexive in English or not?

When I first saw Alex in the school corridor and **1** verliebte mich with him, he didn't even know who I was. But I **2** dachte mir aus a good plan to meet him. His younger sister was in my class, so I **3** lud mich selbst ein to her house. Before I went there I **4** machte mich as beautiful as I could. I **5** machte mir Sorgen that Alex might not be at home, but it was Alex who opened the door for me. Of course when I saw him I **6** fühlte mich really nervous and excited. Maybe that was why I didn't see their cat and fell over it. Anyway, I suddenly **7** fand mich on the floor. I really **8** tat mir weh, but Alex was horrible. He just stood there and laughed at me. In a second my feelings **9** änderten sich, and I **10** entschied mich that I didn't love him any more!

1. fell in love
2. thought of
3. invited myself
4. made myself
5. worried
6. felt
7. found myself
8. hurt myself
9. changed
10. decided

7 Complete what a teenager says with *each other* or *themselves* (→ PB p. 45)

"I don't like it when people show themselves to the whole world on TV! Yesterday I saw a film about a real family where the parents shouted at each other and the kids fought each other all the time. All of them were selfish and only thought of themselves. They never spent time with each other. I wonder what they thought when they saw themselves in the film! I'm glad that in my family we're normally nice to each other."

8 Complete the answers with reflexive forms to stress the subjects (→ PB p. 45)

1. Hey, where's my last sweet? I'm sure there was still one in the bag! Did you eat it?
   – No, I didn't! I think you ate it yourself.
2. What a terrible mess we all made at the twins' party! Who helped them to tidy up?
   – Nobody. After everybody had gone home, they tidied up themselves.
3. What about your girlfriend's ticket at the cinema? Did you buy it?
   – No, I only had enough for my own ticket, so she bought it herself.
4. Mm! This cake is so good! I must find out from your mum how to make it.
   – My mum? It isn't her cake, it's mine! I made it myself.
5. The room you share with your sister is a strange colour, isn't it? Did your parents choose it?
   – No. And my sister and I really like it! We chose it ourselves.
6. Did you get into trouble with your English teacher when you were late?
   – No. He couldn't be angry with me because he was late himself.
7. This film is really boring. Sorry, but we don't think it was a good idea to suggest it.
   – The film wasn't my idea! You two suggested it yourselves.

9 Mediation *(Erwartungshorizont S. 87)*

Your family and an English family have made arrangements to spend the holidays in each other's homes. When you arrive, you find a note. Your English is best, so you must explain the information in it. Write down in German what you can tell your family about the things in the pictures. Use your exercise book.

TIP
Don't try to put every word into German. Just give the important information.

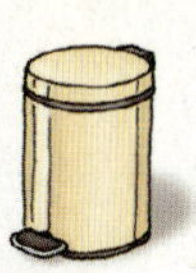

Welcome! Please make yourselves at home here and treat our house as your own. Just a few pieces of information for you:

- There is a list of emergency numbers next to the telephone. Of course we hope you don't need them!
- If you need instructions for the washing machine, TV etc., you will find all the booklets on the shelf in the kitchen.
- Sorry, but the microwave is out of order. The problem only started yesterday, so we haven't had time to get it repaired.
- Rubbish collection day is Tuesday. The neighbours will explain how to sort the rubbish for the green and blue boxes. It would take too long to write it all down here ourselves!
- Feel free to use the bikes in the garage whenever you like. But remember to ride on the left!
- If you see a black cat, please don't encourage it. It isn't ours, but it brings dead mice to us. So we always chase it away.

Enjoy England! We're looking forward to Germany!

TALKWISE

10 Listening: A family problem (→ PB p. 46)

CD 2 – 10

a) *Listen and complete the grid. Write down the suggestions the different people make about how to keep fit. Then make notes about the comments for or against these activities.*

Suggestion:		for:		against:
jog in park	→	cheap – only need trainers	→	boring – no fun in rain
go swimming	→	can walk to swimming	→	often very full – can't swim
ride bikes	→	can visit different places	→	too many hills

b) *Act a role play in groups of 3 or 4. You are a family. You want to get fit together but you all have different ideas about how to do it. Say what you think about each other's ideas, and try to meet halfway.*

11 Put in the correct phrases (→ PB p. 46)

I can see · You've got a point · Don't you think · Can we talk about · I don't mind · How do you feel · That's true, but

Tom: Have you got a minute? *Can we talk about* what I said the other day?

Mother: About a dog? Yes, *I can see* why you'd like one. Dogs are nice.

Father: *That's true, but* they also mean a lot of work.

Tom: I know. *I don't mind* that. I'd like to look after a dog.

Father: But we aren't at home all day. *Don't you think* that's a problem?

Mother: Yes, it is. *You've got a point* there. It isn't fair to leave dogs alone.

Father: But cats don't get so lonely. *How do you feel* about a cat, Tom?

12 Think of a better, friendlier way to answer (→ PB p. 46) *(Erwartungshorizont)*

1. Parent: What a mess in your room! You aren't allowed to go out until you've tidied up.
   Kid: I haven't got time. Anyway, if you don't like the mess, don't look at it.
   My friends are waiting for me. I promise to tidy up when I come home.

2. Parent: Why do you need more pocket money every week? What do you do with it all?
   Kid: That's none of your business!
   I try to spend it carefully, but magazines and CDs are really expensive.

3. Parent: What about a nice family meal at that new restaurant to celebrate your birthday next week?
   Kid: No way! My friends and I have got other plans for my birthday.
   It's a nice idea, but my friends would like to celebrate with me.

4. Parent: Sorry, but you're too young to go to a music festival.
   Kid: It isn't fair. You always say no to everything.
   Maybe I can tell you about it, and then you'll think differently.

13 Your turn: If you could choose (→ PB p. 47) *(Erwartungshorizont)*

1. If you could choose, which famous person would you interview?

– I would interview *David Beckham.*

2. If someone gave you 100 euros to buy something for yourself, what would you buy?

– I would *buy new clothes and CDs.*

3. If you were able to travel back in time, what age or year would you visit?

– *I would visit the Elizabethan Age.*

4. If you had the chance to try a new sport, which one would you try?

– *I would try canoeing.*

14 Put in the correct verbs and forms (→ PB p. 47)

be | do | get on | help | keep | turn

1. I've got an idea, Mum! If we *kept* our bikes in the shed, half of the garage would be empty. 2. And if we *turned* that half into a little room for me, Ben and I wouldn't have to share. 3. I promise that if Ben and I had our own rooms, we *would get on* much better. 4. And of course if we didn't fight so much, it *would be* nicer for you and Dad, too. 5. Please, Mum! If we made a new room for me, it *would help* the whole family. 6. And if we *did* most of the work ourselves, it wouldn't cost much.

15 Make sentences with *If ...* (→ PB p. 48)

Match the correct parts and write down sentences about the Pattersons.

A: Amy • have her own room → she • not fight with Mel so often
B: the girls • not fight so much → their parents • be very happy
C: everybody • help in the house → it • be easier for Mrs Patterson
D: Jake • get up earlier for lunch on Sundays → the others • not have to wait for him
E: Grandpa • live with the family → he • remind them about his wise words

A: If Amy had her own room, she wouldn't fight with Mel so often.

B: If the girls didn't *fight so much, their parents would be very happy.*

C: If *everybody helped in the house, it would be easier for Mrs Patterson.*

D: *If Jake got up earlier for lunch on Sundays, the others wouldn't have to wait for him.*

E: *If Grandpa lived with the family, he would remind them about his wise words* every day.

16 Make helpful suggestions (→ PB p. 48)

a) *Use the ideas on the right to explain what could help with the people's problems.*

Use a dictionary!

Only make important calls!

Join some clubs!

Put up some nice posters!

Train him!

1. "My mobile costs so much to use." – It wouldn't cost so much to use if you only made important calls.

2. "My dog runs away from me all the time." – He wouldn't run away from you all the time if you trained him.

3. "I make so many spelling mistakes." – You wouldn't make so many spelling mistakes if you used a dictionary.

4. "My bedroom looks boring." – It wouldn't look boring if you put up some nice posters.

5. "It's so hard to make new friends." – It wouldn't be so hard if you joined some clubs.

b) *Now use* ***If I were you, …*** *to give the advice in a) in a different way.*
Write in your exercise book. *(Lösungen S. 87)*

Examples: 1. If I were you, I would only make important calls.
2. If I were you, I would …

17 Revision: If-clauses type 1 (→ PB p. 48)

The grid shows different situations when you can use type 1 if-sentences.
Choose the correct ideas to make the example sentences in the grid.

you / make the shelf like this – it / be stronger • you / prepare the vegetables – I / prepare the meat
you / help me with my Maths – I / lend you my CD • you / leave your bag there ✓ – someone / fall over it
you / brush your teeth regularly – they / stay healthy • the weather / be OK tomorrow – I / paint the shed

Use type 1 if-sentences to …	Examples
1. give a warning:	If you leave your bag there, someone will fall over it.
2. suggest how to share work:	If you prepare the vegetables, I'll prepare the meat.
3. talk about plans:	If the weather is OK tomorrow, I'll paint the shed.
4. explain how to do things:	If you make the shelf like this, it will be stronger.
5. get what you want:	If you help me with my Maths, I'll lend you my CD.
6. give reasons for actions:	If you brush your teeth regularly, they will stay healthy.

18 Your turn: What would you have done? (→ PB p. 49)

a) *Write down your answers.*

1. If you had been allowed to stay in bed longer this morning, would you have stayed there or would you have got up at the same time anyway?

   I would have *stayed in bed longer. / I would have got up at the same time anyway.*

2. If your teacher had forgotten to give the class English homework last week, would you have reminded him / her or would you have said nothing?

   I would have reminded him / her. / I would have said nothing. / I wouldn't have said anything.

3. If you had been able to choose your own name when you were born, would you have chosen the name you have got or would you have thought of a different name?

   I would have chosen the name I have got. / I would have thought of a different name.

4. If someone at school had started a fight with you yesterday, would you have got aggressive or would you have walked away?

   I would have got aggressive. / I would have walked away.

b) *Talk in groups. Compare your answers in a). Explain the reasons for your answers.*

19 Go on with what the people say (→ PB p. 49) *(Lösungen S. 87)*

First read what the speakers in the pictures say. Then write type 3 if-sentences to explain what would or wouldn't have happened if the situation had been different. Use your exercise book.

You can start: 1. If you had taken off your trainers, you wouldn't have made the floor dirty!
2. If you hadn't forgotten … *Go on, please.*

LISTENING SKILLS

20 Put in the missing words (→ PB p. 50)

Answerphone: Hello. _I'm_ afraid the person you wish to speak to can't take your _call_ at the moment. If you _would_ like to _leave_ a message, _please_ speak after the _tone_ .

Caller: Hello, _this_ is Mel. I've got a _message_ for Kim. Can you please call me _back_ , Kim? Thanks. _Hope_ to _hear_ from you soon. _Bye_ .

21 Make the dialogue (→ PB p. 50)

Write down who says what in the correct order.

- Great. Thank you very much, Mrs Carter.
- Hello. This is Anne Carter.
- Yes, please. Can you tell him I need to talk about our project?
- You're welcome, Jake. Goodbye.
- Sorry, he isn't in at the moment. Can I give him a message?
- OK. I'll tell him. Then he can call you back.
- Hi, Mrs Carter. It's Jake here. Can I speak to Alex, please?

Mrs Carter: Hello. This is Anne Carter.

Jake: Hi, Mrs Carter. It's Jake here. Can I speak to Alex, please?

Mrs Carter: Sorry, he isn't in at the moment. Can I give him a message?

Jake: Yes, please. Can you tell him I need to talk about our project?

Mrs Carter: OK. I'll tell him. Then he can call you back.

Jake: Great. Thank you very much, Mrs Carter.

Mrs Carter: You're welcome, Jake. Goodbye.

22 Write a phone call (→ PB p. 50) *(Erwartungshorizont S. 88)*

a) *Read the note which Mrs Patterson has written for Amy. Then write the phone call between Nicola Green and Mrs Patterson in your exercise book. The Useful phrases on page 50 in your book can help you.*

b) *Check the phone call which your partner has written. Can you make any suggestions about how to improve it?*

c) *Act the phone calls with your partner. Take turns to play the different roles.*

Message for Amy:
Nicola Green called — has got the flu — can't go to the cinema with you tomorrow.

23 Home alone: Complete the sentences in your own words. (→ PB p. 53) *(EH)*

Scene 1: When Mr and Mrs Patterson go to see Grandpa and leave the children in the house by themselves, Amy and Mel *decide to have a monster party.*

Scene 2: Mr and Mrs Patterson want to show Grandpa a home they have found for him because he *can't look after himself any more.*

Scene 3: They have visited the home but they didn't like it, so Mr and Mrs Patterson *invite Grandpa to live with the family.*

Scene 4: Amy and Mel get a shock when their parents *suddenly arrive with Grandpa.*

Scene 5: Mr and Mrs Patterson are angry with the children about the party in the hobby room, but Grandpa *thinks it is great.*

24 Do you think it is good when grandparents live with the family? (→ PB p. 53)

a) *Write notes about why it might be good or not so good when grandparents live with the family.*

b) *Work in groups of five or six. Use your notes from a) to talk about the question in the heading. Then vote for or against the ideas.*

c) *Choose a speaker. He / she tells the class what the group voted for and why.*

25 A play puzzle (→ PB p. 53)

1. People who watch a play do this if they enjoy it.
2. You use this word for all the people who act in a play.
3. This falls at the end of a play.
4. This person tells the actors what to do.
5. Actors must do this before they can perform a play.
6. This word tells you that the actor is a woman.
7. An actor wears this for his or her role.
8. These are all the things actors use on stage.
9. This word means all the people who watch a play.
10. This is the name of the family in 'Home alone'.

1	A P **P** L A U D
2	C **A** S T
3	C U R **T** A I N
4	D I R E C **T** O R
5	R E H **E** A R S E
6	A C T **R** E S S
7	C O **S** T U M E
8	P R **O** P S
9	A U D I E **N** C E
10	PATTERSON

26 Writing texts: A dream room (→ PB p. 53) *(EH S. 88)*

a) *Imagine your dream room. What is in it? What you can do there? Collect ideas and interesting words and phrases.*

b) *Now use your ideas from a) to describe your dream room. Write a text of 100 – 120 words. Don't forget to check it when you have finished. Use your exercise book.*

27 Tandem activity: Find the differences in the pictures (→ PB p. 54)

Work with a partner. Choose picture A or picture B. Don't look at your partner's picture. Take turns to describe the people in the family and find four differences for every person.

A

You describe the mother and the son. Give as many details as you can so that your partner can find out what is different. When your partner describes the father and the daughter, listen carefully and draw a circle round the differences in your picture. You are allowed to ask questions if the information is not clear.

You describe the father and the daughter. Give as many details as you can so that your partner can find out what is different. When your partner describes the mother and the son, listen carefully and draw a circle round the differences in your picture. You are allowed to ask questions if the information is not clear.

B

28 Complete the sentences with a noun from the same word family

1. He *invited* me to the party although I hadn't expected to get an invitation.
2. I would never call myself a *lucky* person because I've had bad luck so often in my life.
3. The twins wear *different* clothes, but that is the only difference you can see between them.
4. I like *vegetables* but I enjoy meat, too, so I wouldn't want to become a vegetarian.
5. Nobody was in when I *phoned*, so I left a message on the answerphone.
6. If my parents can't *decide* where to go for our holidays, I'll be happy to make the decision myself!

29 Put in the correct verbs with *up*

1. look up words in a dictionary. 2. He decided to split up with his girlfriend. 3. What time do you get up in the mornings? 4. My room is a mess because I never tidy up. 5. Sports champions fight to the end and never give up. 6. If you hold up your hand, it shows that you want to speak. 7. Some parents pick up their kids in the car after school.

30 Underline the correct form for the sentence (→ PB p. 55)

1. I (remember me • remember myself • remember) a brilliant monster party I went to last year.
2. We all (made us • made ourselves • made each other) monster costumes for the party.
3. It was so funny when we arrived and (saw • saw each other • saw us) with scary faces.
4. Everybody (enjoyed themselves • enjoyed each other • enjoyed) at the party.
5. All the food and drink was on a table where we could (help each other • help us • help ourselves).
6. A green monster ate so much that he (felt • felt himself • felt him) sick – and became even greener!
7. Two other monsters at the party fell in love and started to (kiss themselves • kiss them • kiss)!

31 Make sentences with *would* (→ PB p. 55)

Grandpa Patterson and the kids are talking about what they would do if they were alone at home and heard a strange noise upstairs. Look at the pictures and write down what they say.

1. Amy: I would *call the police on my mobile.*
2. Jake: I *would jump out of the window.*
3. Mel: *I would hide behind the sofa.*
4. Grandpa: *I would go upstairs with a cricket bat.*

32 Complete these if-sentences with the correct verb forms (→ PB p. 55)

First look at the other verb. Then you will know if the sentence is type 1, type 2 or type 3.

1. If you *had looked* (look) after my camera, you wouldn't have broken it!
2. If you give me the chance, I *will tell* (tell) you what happened.
3. If you *don't shout* (not shout) at me, I won't shout at you.
4. If you *knew* (know) the facts, you wouldn't be so angry with me.
5. If you had explained right away, I *wouldn't have gone* (not go) so crazy.
6. If I had the money, I *would buy* (buy) you a new camera.

⟨A series of unfortunate events⟩

Violet, Klaus and Sunny are intelligent, charming[1] and resourceful[2], but they are also extremely unlucky. In this first book about the Baudelaire children, we learn about how things started to go wrong. All the other volumes are based on this first tragedy.

Book the First – The Bad Beginning

The three Baudelaire children lived with their parents in an enormous mansion[3] at the heart of a dirty and busy city, and occasionally their parents gave them permission to take a rickety trolley – the word "rickety,", you probably know, here means "unsteady" or "likely to collapse" – alone to the seashore, where they would spend the day as a sort of vacation as long as they were home for dinner. This particular morning it was gray and cloudy, which didn't bother the Baudelaire youngsters one bit. When it was hot and sunny, Briny Beach was crowded with tourists and it was impossible to find a good place to lay one's blanket. On gray and cloudy days, the Baudelaires had the beach to themselves to do what they liked.

Violet Baudelaire, the eldest, liked to skip rocks[4]. Like most fourteen-year-olds, she was right-handed, so the rocks skipped farther across the murky[5] water when Violet used her right hand than when she used her left. As she skipped rocks, she was looking out at the horizon and thinking about an invention[6] she wanted to build.

Anyone who knew Violet well could tell she was thinking hard, because her long hair was tied up in a ribbon to keep it out of her eyes. Violet had a real knack for[7] inventing and building strange devices[8], so her brain was often filled with images of pulleys[9], levers[10], and gears[11], and she never wanted to be distracted by something as trivial as her hair. This morning she was thinking about how to construct a device that could retrieve[12] a rock after you had skipped it into the ocean.

Klaus Baudelaire, the middle child, and the only boy, liked to examine creatures in tide-pools[13]. Klaus was a little older than twelve and wore glasses, which made him look intelligent. He was intelligent. The Baudelaire parents had an enormous library in their mansion, a room filled with thousands of books on nearly every subject. Being only twelve, Klaus of course had not read all of the books in the Baudelaire library, but he had a great many of them and had retained a lot of the information from his readings. He knew how to tell an alligator from a crocodile. He knew who killed Julius Caesar. And he knew much about the tiny, slimy animals found at Briny Beach, which he was examining now.

Sunny Baudelaire, the youngest, liked to bite things. She was an infant[14], and very small for her age, scarcely larger than a boot. What she lacked in size, however, she made up for with the size and sharpness of her four teeth. Sunny was at an age where one mostly speaks in a series of unintelligible[15] shrieks. […]For instance, this morning she was saying "Gack!" over and over, which probably meant, "Look at that mysterious figure emerging from the fog!"

Sure enough, in the distance along the misty shore of Briny Beach there could be seen a tall figure striding toward the Baudelaire children.

As the figure reached them, the children saw with relief that it was not anybody frightening at all, but somebody they knew: Mr Poe. Mr Poe was a friend of Mr and Mrs Baudelaire's whom the children had met many times at dinner parties. […]

"Yes, it is a nice day," Mr Poe said absently, staring out at the empty beach. "I'm afraid I have some very bad news for you children."

"Your parents," Mr Poe said, "have perished in a terrible fire".

The children didn't say anything.

"They perished," Mr Poe said, "in a fire that destroyed the entire[16] house. I'm very, very sorry to tell you this, my dears."

[…] "'Perished,'" Mr. Poe said, "means 'killed.'"

adapted from: *A series of unfortunate events* by Lemony Snicket

[1]**charming** ('tʃɑ:mɪŋ) = bezaubernd • [2]**resourceful** (rɪ'zɔ:sfl) = einfallsreich • [3]**mansion** ('mænʃn) = Villa • [4]**(to) skip rocks** (skip 'rɒks) = Steine über das Wasser springen lassen • [5]**murky** ('mɜ:ki) = trüb • [6]**invention** (ɪn'venʃn) = Erfindung • [7]**(to) have a knack for sth** (ˌhæv‿ə 'ŋæk fə) = ein Talent/Händchen für etw. haben • [8]**device** (dɪ'vaɪs) = Gerät; Vorrichtung • [9]**pulley** ('pʊli) = Flaschenzug • [10]**lever** ('li:və) = Hebel • [11]**gear** (gɪə) = Zahnrad • [12]**(to) retrieve** (rɪ'tri:v) = zurückholen • [13]**tide-pool** ('taɪd pu:l) = *Wasserloch am Strand bei Ebbe* • [14]**infant** ('ɪnfənt) = Kleinkind • [15]**unintelligible** (ˌʌnɪn'telɪdʒəbl) = unverständlich • [16]**entire** (ɪn'taɪə) = gesamt, ganz

Unit 4 The UK on the move

1 A regional crossword (→ PB p. 58)

1 E		2 W	I	N	G			3 B	
X		E				4 R		I	
5 C	U	L	T	U	R	E		R	
H		S				G		T	
A		H				I		H	
N						O		P	
G		6 R	E	C	E	N	T	L	Y
E								A	
								C	
7 L	A	N	D	S	C	A	P	E	

Across: →
2. A bird has got two …s to fly.
5. Every country has got its own traditional …
6. Not long ago
7. Wales is famous for its wild … of mountains and lakes.

Down: ↓
1. When pupils from different countries visit each other
2. People from Wales speak …
3. He was born in London. It's his …
4. Part of a country

2 Listening: Regional voices (→ PB p. 59)

Underline the wrong words and correct the sentences.

1. a) Swansea is the <u>largest</u> city in Wales. *Swansea is the second largest city in Wales.*
   b) A quarter of Welsh people speak <u>English</u>. *A quarter of Welsh people speak Welsh.*
   c) The Welsh have got good <u>football</u> players. *The Welsh have got good rugby players.*
2. a) Reading is in the <u>north</u> of England. *Reading is in the south of England.*
   b) It takes <u>two hours</u> to get to London. *It takes forty minutes to get to London.*
   c) The landscape looks <u>grey and sad</u>. *The landscape looks green and rich and friendly.*
3. a) The Industrial Revolution started in <u>London</u>. *The Industrial Revolution started in the North.*
   b) Some old factories are <u>schools</u> now. *Some old factories are museums or flats now.*
   c) People from Manchester are proud of all the <u>invitations</u>. *People from Manchester are proud of all the inventions.*

3 Your turn: A postcard from Germany (→ PB p. 59) *(Erwartungshorizont S. 88)*

Write a postcard from your region to a friend in England in your exercise book.

4 Rhona's world (→ PB p. 60)

*Fill in the definite article **the** where it is necessary.*

1. Rhona likes ___–___ music.
2. Shirin and Rhona don't like ___the___ music that David listens to.
3. But ___the___ time they spend together is always a lot of fun!
4. For Rhona, ___–___ love and ___–___ friendship are really important.
5. ___–___ life is interesting for Shirin because her family moved house a year ago.
6. ___The___ friendship with Shirin is very important for Rhona.
7. Rhona thinks that ___–___ time goes quickly when you're talking with a friend.

5 Write about people you know (→ PB p. 61) *(Erwartungshorizont)*

person	job	goes to work	reads the newspaper / listens to the radio / watches TV / jogs / ...
dad • mum uncle • aunt neighbour best friend's father ...	doctor shop assistant nurse • teacher manager taxi driver ...	bus car train bike ...	before after at breakfast lunch tea ...

1. My dad is a doctor. He goes to work by car. He reads the newspaper before breakfast.
2. My mum *is a nurse. She goes to work by bus. She listens to the radio after lunch.*
3. *My aunt is a shop assistant. She goes to work by train. She watches TV after tea.*
4. *My best friend's mother is a taxi driver. She goes to work by car. She jogs before breakfast.*
5. *Our neighbour is a teacher. He goes to work by bike. He reads books after lunch.*
6. *My uncle is a manager. He goes to work by taxi. He talks a lot at breakfast.*

TIP

Remember that we often use articles in English and German differently!

6 Adjectives as nouns (→ PB p. 61)

disabled | English | rich ✓ | young | sad | famous | poor | nervous

Use these adjectives to complete the sentences from a TV guide.

1. **Different worlds:** A look at the different lifestyles of the rich and the poor.
2. **Kidshop:** Saturday morning fun for the young.
3. **Startalk:** More interviews with the famous.
4. **Smile!** A report about clowns who help the sad.
5. **Our neighbours in the south:** A group of Scots discuss the English.
6. **Night of horror:** Not a film for the nervous.
7. **Wheelchairs welcome:** Holidays for the disabled.

7 How to: Meet new people (→ PB p. 61) *(Erwartungshorizont)*

You meet someone new at a party. What can you say? What could the other person say? Fill in the speech bubbles. The Useful phrases on page 61 in your book can help you.

8 Revision: Possessive pronouns (→ PB p. 61)

Fill in the correct possessive pronouns in Rhona's message on David's answerphone.

Hello, David. This is Rhona. How was your weekend? Mine was OK, but I missed you. Thanks for inviting Shirin and me to see a concert of yours. Well – we liked it. You know, your friends are much more traditional than ours, but that's OK. Listen, I've found an MP3 player in my bag and it's not mine. Is it yours? If not, can you please ask your friend Jason if it's his? It can't be Shirin's because hers looks different. Bye, David. See you tomorrow!

TALKWISE

9 Tandem activity: Helping someone (→ PB p. 62)

A blind[1] woman wants to cross the road. Work with a partner. Ask questions and find answers. Check your partner's sentences. The Useful phrases on page 62 in your book can help you.

A

1. *Can I help* you across the road?
2. Oh, that's very kind of you.
3. *Shall I* take your arm?
4. Yes, please. There are so many people everywhere.
5. OK, it's green. You needn't hurry. Just *take your time.*
6. Thank you. Could you show me the supermarket, please?
7. *No problem.* Here we are.
8. Thanks a lot. You've been a great help!
9. You're welcome. *Goodbye.*

B

1. Can I help you across the road?
2. Oh, that's *very kind of you.*
3. Shall I take your arm?
4. Yes, *please.* There are so many people everywhere.
5. OK, it's green. You needn't hurry. Just take your time.
6. Thank you. *Could you* show me the supermarket, please?
7. No problem. Here we are.
8. Thanks a lot. You've *been a great help!*
9. You're welcome. Goodbye.

10 Apologizing to someone (→ PB p. 62) *(Erwartungshorizont)*

Work with a partner. What would you and your partner say in these situations?

1. You took your partner's workbook home, so he/she couldn't do his/her homework.

You: *I'm really sorry I took your workbook home.*

Your partner: *Never mind. But please be more careful next time.*

2. You forgot your partner's birthday and remembered it a week later.

You: *I'm terribly sorry I forgot your birthday. Here's a little present for you.*

Your partner: *No problem. And thanks for the present!*

3. You told a friend that your partner's hair looks terrible. Your partner heard you.

You: *I'm very sorry. I didn't mean to be rude.*

Your partner: *That's OK. Let's just forget it.*

[1]**blind** [blaɪnd] = blind

11 Mediation: A visit to Liverpool (→ PB p. 63)

You and your brother are staying with your English friend Arun in Liverpool. Arun's family is from India. Your brother does not speak English very well, so you help him.

Brother: Seine Familie ist viel größer als unsere!

You: My brother says *your family is much bigger than ours.*

Arun: Yes, I've got many relatives. And they would like to meet my friends from Germany!

You: Er hat *viele Verwandte. Und sie würden gerne seine Freunde aus Deutschland kennen lernen.*

Brother: Bitte frag ihn, was sie gerade essen.

You: *He asks what you are eating.*

Arun: Oh, that's curry, Indian food. Please try some.

You: *Das ist Curry, indisches Essen. Er bittet Dich, es zu probieren.*

Brother: Ja gerne. Seine Tanten sprechen eine andere Sprache. Welche Sprache ist das?

You: *Yes, he would like to try some. Which language are your aunts speaking?*

Arun: That's Punjabi, an Indian language. But I don't speak it very well. I usually speak English.

You: *Das ist Punjabi, eine indische Sprache. Aber Arun spricht sie nicht sehr gut. Er spricht normalerweise Englisch.*

12 Revision: Adjective or adverb? (→ PB p. 63)

1. Shirin has got a *big* (big) and *loud* (loud) family.
2. Aunt Zeba cooks *well* (good). Everyone eats her food *greedily* (greedy[1]), but Rhona tries it *carefully* (careful) because she doesn't know Asian food.
3. Shirin's aunts and uncles speak an *interesting* (interesting) language, Punjabi.
4. Shirin's cousin Tariq is very *nice* (nice).
5. There are many *cool* (cool) bands in Manchester. They play their instruments *brilliantly* (brilliant) and dance *well* (good).
6. The girls listen to a *great* (great) busker and cheer *happily* (happy). Shirin says: "I think he will be *famous* (famous) soon."

[1] **greedy** ['gri:di] = gierig

13 Moving house (→ PB p. 64)

Fill in an adjective or an adverb.

1. Jane and Bob moved house yesterday. In the morning, Bob looked *tired* (tired).
2. He was *excited* (excited), but he felt *good* (good).
3. Jane seemed *happy* (happy), too.
4. They *quickly* (quick) brushed their teeth and got dressed.
5. Their breakfast tasted *great* (great) and they ate *quietly* (quiet).
6. They got *nervous* (nervous) when their relatives came in to take the boxes.
7. Everybody worked *hard* (hard).
8. In the evening they went to a restaurant. The food smelled *nice* (nice) and they ate *hungrily* (hungry).

14 Your turn: Different situations (→ PB p. 64)

a) *How would you feel in these situations? Think of adjectives.* ***(Erwartungshorizont)***

1. in a new class

shy

2. at my first snowboarding course

scared

3. before a big presentation

nervous

4. with my exchange family

curious

5. at a friend's house

hungry

6. after a long trip on the coach

tired

b) *Choose one of the situations and write a paragraph about it in your exercise book.* ***(EH S. 88)***

15 Rhona's week (→ PB p. 65)

What will Rhona have done by the end of the week? Use the future perfect.

1. She <u>will have gone</u> (go) to the cinema with David.
2. She <u>will have spoken to</u> (speak to) Shirin about David's hobby.
3. She <u>will have told</u> (tell) her parents about her boyfriend.
4. She <u>will have written</u> (write) in her diary.
5. She <u>will have bought</u> (buy) a Welsh CD.
6. She <u>will have phoned</u> (phone) David.

16 Listening: After the Beatles Story (→ PB p. 65)

Listen to Rhona and Shirin's conversation about the Beatles Story. Listen again and fill in the grid.

Question	Shirin	Rhona
1. How does the sentence end?	The Beatles were the first boy band!	I think their hair looked cool.
2. Most famous Beatle? Why?	John Lennon – because he was killed.	Paul McCartney – because he worked alone after the band split up.
3. Other band members? Which instrument?	George Harrison lead guitar	Ringo Starr drums
4. Favourite songs?	Yellow submarine Yesterday	She Loves You Michelle
5. Best part of the museum?	big yellow submarine photos of the band members	John Lennon's glasses[1] George Harrison's first guitar

[1] **glasses** ['glɑːsɪz] = Brille

READING SKILLS

17 Factual texts (→ PB p. 66)

1 Skimming *(Erwartungshorizont)*

Read this text quickly and underline keywords.
Write down in one sentence what the text is about.

The text is about Oxford, a famous university town

in the south of England with many tourist activities.

2 Scanning

Look at the text again. Is there any information about these things? Just say "yes" or "no".

a) free time activities	*yes*	b) actors and singers	*no*	c) public transport	*no*
d) 1st May	*yes*	e) history	*yes*	f) famous university[1]	*yes*

You have probably heard of Oxford, a city in the south of England in the county[2] of Oxfordshire. This town is famous in the world for its important university which is over 750 years old. Many students from all round the world go to Oxford. For example, the University of Tübingen in Baden-Württemberg has got an exchange programme with Oxford. For tourists and visitors, there are many things to do. You can go on a boat trip on the rivers Cherwell and Thames, visit the old libraries and museums, go to a nice restaurant or enjoy shopping on High Street. Oxford is also called "the city of dreaming spires[3]" because it has got many towers and churches. Oxford's history is interesting. The Romans built roads, the Saxons built the first cathedral[4], the Normans built Oxford castle in 1072 and Richard the Lionheart was born at Beaumont Palace in 1157. Every year on 1st May at 6 am, a lot of people come together to hear the choir of Magdalen college[5] sing from the top of their church tower. The tradition of May Day Singing began in the 17th century. After the singing, crazy students jumped into the River Cherwell from Magdalen Bridge. But the water is only 1–2 metres deep[6], so many students broke their legs. This is why the bridge was closed in 2006.

After the singing the students usually have breakfast picnics in the college gardens.

3 Collect Information

Make a list of topics from the text. Then write down in your exercise book in a few sentences what the text tells you about life in Oxford. *(Erwartungshorizont S. 88)*

university (750 years old), *students from all round the world,*

exchange programme with Tübingen in Baden-Württemberg

tourist activities (boat trip, old libraries and museums, restaurants, shopping)

history (Romans, Saxons, Normans, Richard the Lionheart)

1st May (May Day Singing, students jumping into river, breakfast picnics)

[1] **university** [ˌjuːnɪˈvɜːsəti] = Universität • [2] **county** [ˈkaʊnti] = Grafschaft • [3] **spire** [ˈspaɪə] = Turmspitze • [4] **cathedral** [kəˈθiːdrl] = Kathedrale • [5] **college** [ˈkɒlɪdʒ] = *eine von insgesamt 39 selbstständigen Einheiten der* University of Oxford • [6] **deep** [diːp] = tief

18 A quiz about British regions (→ PB p. 67)

Read the text "Changing places" again and do this quiz.

1. What is the Welsh name for 'Swansea'? *Abertawe* ✓
2. How many skateparks are there in Swansea? *nine*
3. What is special about the National Waterfront Museum in Swansea? *It's interactive.*
4. What is the name of the river you can cross by ferry? *The Mersey*
5. What did Joseph Williamson build in Liverpool in the 1820s? *The Williamson Tunnels*
6. Which sports club comes from Anfield Road in Liverpool? *Liverpool Football Club*
7. What is another word for Standard English? *BBC English*
8. Who spends her weekends at Windsor castle? *The Queen*

19 The next time (→ PB p. 67) *(Erwartungshorizont)*

Which places would Wayne, Michael and Rhona visit if they went to Swansea, Liverpool and Reading a second time? Why do you think so?

1. Wayne would *go to the Leisure Centre Skatepark because it is the best he saw.*
2. Michael would *go on a ferry trip because it is fun and does not cost much.*
3. Rhona would *go to a festival at the Rivermead Leisure Complex to show her boyfriend some good folk music.*

20 Writing texts: A family holiday in the UK (→ PB p. 68)

a) *You and your family want to spend your summer holiday in the UK. Your parents asked you to choose an interesting town. Use an Internet search engine to find a nice place.*

b) *Use the Reading skills you learnt on page 66 in your book to find out about free time activities, the town's history, the people who live there etc.*

c) *Now write about your favourite holiday town in your exercise book. Write:* *(EH S. 88)*

- what the place is
- where in the UK it is
- why it is a good place for a summer holiday
- what the people in your family (you, your mum, dad, brother, sister) can do there
- what is not so good about it.

21 A word web

VOCABULARY SKILLS

Find ten tourist words in the grid on the right and make a word web.

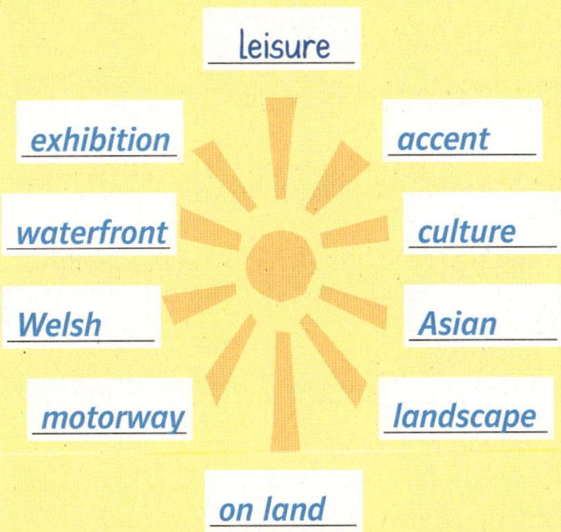

A B C D E F G H I

L	A	N	D	S	C	A	P	E	L	T
E	C	W	P	B	U	A	F	P	C	X
I	C	A	O	N	L	A	N	D	P	H
S	E	U	M	O	T	O	R	W	A	Y
U	N	D	K	U	U	W	E	L	S	H
R	T	O	L	B	R	W	O	T	I	Q
E	E	N	Z	M	E	Q	F	V	A	T
T	W	A	T	E	R	F	R	O	N	T
Q	S	C	A	H	W	Q	E	L	J	R
Z	Y	N	P	T	A	L	Z	C	I	W
E	E	X	H	I	B	I	T	I	O	N

22 Tariq's clothes (→ PB p. 70)

*Complete the text with **pair(s) of . . . .***

Shirin's cousin Tariq has got four pairs of jeans (jeans) and many pairs of socks (socks). In his free time, he usually wears a pair of trainers (trainers), but he must wear a normal pair of black shoes (black shoes) to school. For his birthday, his mum will buy him a cool pair of boots (boots) and a new pair of sunglasses (sunglasses). He already owns eight pairs of sunglasses (sunglasses). In summer, he likes to wear a T-shirt and a pair of shorts (shorts). And when he goes swimming, he usually takes two pairs of goggles (goggles) because his best friend always forgets his own pair of goggles (goggles).

23 Listening: Sounds and spelling (→ PB p. 70)

Listen and tick ✔ which word you hear.

1. a) ☐ woman b) ☑ women
2. a) ☑ quite b) ☐ quiet
3. a) ☐ just b) ☑ gist
4. a) ☑ love b) ☐ laugh
5. a) ☑ earn b) ☐ own
6. a) ☑ average b) ☐ every age
7. a) ☑ cult b) ☐ cold
8. a) ☐ coal b) ☑ cool
9. a) ☐ carry b) ☑ curry

24 With or without *the*? (→ PB p. 71)

1. You can easily get from London to Oxford by __–__ train.
2. __The__ bus to Oxford leaves from Victoria Station. The trip takes about one hour.
3. You can also go by __–__ car, but there is always a lot of traffic on the motorway.
4. There are many things to do for __the__ young. They often go to discos like Park End.
   __The__ music they play there is very popular with teenagers.
5. __The__ rich can go shopping in Little Clarendon Street, an expensive place in town.
6. Some people eat __–__ lunch at a restaurant. __The__ lunch at "The King's Arms" tastes great.

25 Future perfect

What will you have done by the end of this school year? Use the future perfect.

1. I __will have talked__ (talk) about British regions and other subjects.
2. I __will have read__ (read) many English stories.
3. I __will have written__ (write) my own texts.
4. I __will have found out__ (find out) a lot about towns in the UK from the Internet.
5. I __will have watched__ (watch) an English film.
6. I __will have understood__ (understand) the future perfect!

26 Adjective or adverb? (→ PB p. 71)

1. Oxford's traditions on May Day seem __interesting__ (interesting).
2. Visitors can see __perfectly__ (perfect) if they arrive before 6 am.
3. The choir of Magdalen college sings __beautifully__ (beautiful).
4. Everyone is __quiet__ (quiet) and listens __carefully__ (careful).
5. The students who jump into the river seem __crazy__ (crazy), but the police stay __calm__ (calm).
6. When the students feel __hungry__ (hungry) they go to the college gardens.
7. The breakfast there tastes __great__ (great).
8. Kids run around in the gardens and play __happily__ (happy).

⟨Revision for tests⟩ Unit 3–4

1 Complete the *if*-sentences

A few days ago Grandpa's cleaning lady phoned the Pattersons. If she *hadn't talked* (not talk) to Mr and Mrs Patterson, they *wouldn't have looked for* (not look for) an old people's home. They are not sure what is best. "If Grandpa Patterson *is* (be) too old to look after himself, he *can live* (live) with us," said Mr Patterson. "If he *comes/came* (come) to live with us, he and the children *will/would enjoy* (enjoy) themselves," Mrs Patterson replied.

They spoke to him and said: "We've found a nice home for you. Everybody says it's nice, but if you *don't like* (not like) it, we *will take* (take) you back." So they all went to the home and had lunch there. The food was really bad! If they *hadn't eaten* (not eat) lunch at the home, they *wouldn't have found out* (not find out) how bad the food was. If I *were* (be) Grandpa Patterson, I *wouldn't go* (not go) to that old people's home. Would you?

2 Listening: Telephone messages *(Lösungen / Erwartungshorizont S. 88)*

a) *When Rhona turns on her mobile there are three messages for her. Listen to them. What are the important points? (Who? What? Where? When?) Write them in your exercise book.*
b) *Write a message for your answerphone/voice mail when you cannot answer the phone yourself.*

3 An e-mail to a tourist information centre *(Erwartungshorizont S. 88)*

a) *You are doing an English project 'Visit Britain'. What part of Britain do you want to visit? What do you want to know? Make notes.*
b) *Write an e-mail to a tourist information centre in the region where you want to go. Say who you are, where you are from, what you want and why. Use your notes from a).*

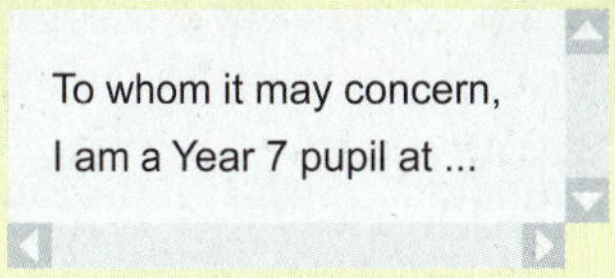

4 Helping and apologizing *(Erwartungshorizont S. 88)*

What can the people say in these situations? Look at the Useful phrases on page 62 in your book and write two-line dialogues in your exercise book. Use different phrases if you can.

1. Aunt Zeba is carrying some heavy plates and can't open the kitchen door.
2. Rhona opens the door and hits Shirin, who is standing behind it.
3. Rhona is looking at a street map of Liverpool. A boy asks her what she is looking for.
4. A young boy doesn't look where he is going and bumps into Rhona outside the shops in Albert Dock. He apologizes.

5 Reading factual texts: Multicultural music *(Erwartungshorizont S. 89)*

a) ***Skim** the text. What is the topic and what are the most important points?*

b) ***Scan** the text. Does it give you information about the points in the box on the right? If it does, make notes.*

- musical instruments
- history
- geography
- free time activities
- famous people
- tourist industry

Bhangra started in the 1970s and has now become a very popular form of music in Britain, America and other parts of the world. It has brought Asian and Western music together and is played in clubs and discos. Young people like it because it is fun to listen and dance to, but it is also still an important part of traditional[1] Indian regional culture.

Bhangra started in the fields of the Punjab region in what is now west Pakistan and north-west India. The farmers danced and sang songs about village life while they were working in the fields. It helped them to forget how hard the work was. Later people also danced and sang these songs when a man and woman got married and when they celebrated the New Year or other festivals.

The two most important instruments are the *tumbi* (see photo on the right), an instrument with one string[2], and the *dhol* (see photo on the left), a drum that you play by hitting it with two sticks. Although the *tumbi* has only got one string, it takes a very long time to learn how to play it.

Kuldip Manak was one of the fathers of modern Bhangra. He grew up in a musical family in Punjab – the home of Bhangra. Malkit Singh (on the right in the photo above), another popular Bhangra star, says: "Kuldip Manak was one of my heroes when I was growing up." But Bhangra is changing all the time. Ask Bally Sagoo. He was the opening act when Michael Jackson played in Bombay. He says Bhangra is "a bit of Indian drums, a bit of the Indian sound and heavy, funky[3] Western drum sounds."

He grew up in Birmingham and is now a really famous Bhangra star who has mixed traditional Punjabi music with Western music like soul and reggae. Bhangra is really multicultural music.

The great interest in Bollywood[4] is another reason why Bhangra has become so popular all over the world. Listen to some Bhangra and you will hear why, too.

c) ***Writing texts:** Choose one of these activities.*

1. *Write a short introduction to a radio programme about Bhangra music. Use your notes from a) and b). Start your programme like this:* This week we are going to talk about and listen to Bhangra. What exactly is Bhangra music? Well, …
2. *Make a poster about Bhangra. Use a search engine to find information and pictures about Bhangra on the Internet. Write short texts for any photos you use. Think carefully about the layout so that others can read it easily when it is on your classroom wall.*

[1]**traditional** [trəˈdɪʃnl]= traditionell • [2]**string** [strɪŋ] = Saite • [3]**funky** [ˈfʌŋki] = irre, flippig • [4]**Bollywood** [ˈbɒliwʊd] = *Indiens Filmindustrie in Mumbay (Bombay)*

Unit 5 Media messages

1 A quiz: What media type are you? (→ PB p. 76) *(Testauswertung S. 89)*

Answer the questions. Then look at page 87 of this Workbook to find out what media type you are.

1. You watch TV
   a) up to 2 hours a day. ☐
   b) more than 3 hours a day. ☐
   c) on some days, not on others. ☐
2. You watch soap operas
   a) because the characters are like good friends. ☐
   b) because they are fun. ☐
   c) but not very often. ☐
3. You watch sports programmes on TV
   a) because you can talk to your friends at school about them. ☐
   b) because you do sports yourself. ☐
   c) but you don't do sports yourself. ☐
4. You listen to music
   a) when you're alone. ☐
   b) all the time when you're not watching TV. ☐
   c) on radio and TV programmes with news about stars. ☐
5. You use your mobile
   a) to listen to music. ☐
   b) to surf on the Internet. ☐
   c) to phone and text friends. ☐

6. When you want to discuss things with friends, you
   a) phone them. ☐
   b) suggest a place to meet. ☐
   c) send e-mails or chat online. ☐
7. The Internet is useful for you because you can
   a) download music (cheaper than CDs). ☐
   b) find information for your homework. ☐
   c) surf all kinds of websites all day. ☐
8. You buy magazines
   a) if you see one which is very interesting for you. ☐
   b) but not very often, because you don't like texts. ☐
   c) and lend them to friends later. ☐

2 Listening: On the radio (→ PB p. 77)

a) *Listen to the three programmes. Find a title for each conversation and write it down.*

1. *A road accident with pigs* 2. *Find the song* 3. *Stars, celebs and music*

b) *What kind of programmes are they? Which words and phrases tell you this?*

Kind of programme	Words and phrases
1. *news programme*	*This morning … there was … When the police arrived, … It took four hours …*
2. *show for listeners at home*	*Hi there, listeners … Got your phones/ears ready? … the first question … Hello? … Sorry, …*
3. *commercial for programme*	*Listen to … on Sunday evenings … our awesome special from 7 to 9 pm …*

3 How can this girl become a star? (→ PB p. 79)

Use the present passive.

1. The girl's agent is phoned. — phone girl's agent
2. The girl's photo *is sent to a Casting Director.* — send girl's photo to Casting Director
3. The girl *is informed about the casting.* — inform girl about casting
4. *Some scenes are acted.* — act some scenes
5. *The girl is chosen for the role.* — choose girl for role
6. *The film is watched by many people.* — watch film by many people
7. *The girl's face is seen in every magazine.* — see girl's face in every magazine
8. *The girl is invited to Hollywood.* — invite girl to Hollywood

4 Topham: 0 – Burton: 2 (→ PB p. 79)

Add the missing verbs in this report. Use the past passive.

An exciting football match *was shown* (show) on TV yesterday afternoon. The Burton players *were cheered* (cheer) by 10,000 fans, and the match *was watched* (watch) by a crowd of 25,000. In the first half the referee *was kicked* (kick) by a Topham player, and the match *was stopped* (stop) for five minutes. At half time the score was still 0 : 0, and the Burton players *were told* (tell) to try harder. In the last five minutes of the match two goals *were scored* (score) for Burton by Tim Jenkins. Tim *was interviewed* (interview) on TV later that evening. "I *was helped* (help) by our great fans," he said.

5 Is everything ready for the scene? (→ PB p. 79) *(Lösungen S. 89)*

The director of a daily soap is preparing to film a scene in a café.
This is what he says:

Now everything is ready. What has been done?
Write the sentences in your exercise book.
Use the present perfect passive

Example: 1. The actors and actresses have been called.

1 Call the actors and actresses, please!

2 Put knives and forks on the tables.

3 Find a chair for my assistant, please!

4 Check everybody's make-up.

5 Close the door!

6 Tell Gloria her costume looks great!

6 Make your own soap (→ PB p. 79)

Class 8JM are making a soap for their school project. Here is part of the script. Put in the simple past passive or the present perfect passive of the right verbs.

TIP
Look for the signal words!
Simple past: last ..., ... ago, ...
Present perfect: yet, already, ...

break | call | check | see (2x) | give | steal | wake up

Doreen: Oh no! My jewellery isn't here! It *has been stolen* !

I'm so sad! That gold watch *was given* to me by Eddie five years ago.

Julie: Don't worry. – The police *have* already *been called*.

Doreen: I *was woken up* at 2 am by an unusual noise. Maybe –

Julie: Yes! Sally says two strange people *were seen* outside the house yesterday evening. *Were* any windows *broken* last night?

Doreen: I'm not sure. They *have* not *been checked* yet.

Julie: Well, our Jimmy wasn't the thief this time. – He *was seen* at Leroy's Disco last night!

7 Tandem activity: Matt's first day as a TV star (→ PB p. 80)

Matt is talking to his friend Dominic after his first day as "Justin" in "EastEnders". Decide who is Matt and who is Dominic. Change the underlined active sentences into the passive.

Dominic

1. What • happen • when • you • arrive • studio?
(I was welcomed by the director.)
2. When • you • meet • other actors?
(I was taken to meet them at once by a nice girl).
3. I guess • lots of people, equipment. • you • very nervous?
(Yes, I was! At first I couldn't / didn't remember my script).

(Change roles: You are Matt now.)

Matt

4. (What did they do then?)
They filmed that scene again • OK • second time
5. (Were you able to see yourself in the new film?)
Yes, they showed us the film • before • we • leave • studio. I • like • it

Matt

1. (What happened when you arrived at the studio?)
The director welcomed me.
2. (When did you meet the other actors?)
A nice girl took me to meet them at once.
3. (I guess there were lots of people and equipment. Were you very nervous?)
Yes. • At first • I • not remember • my script.

(Change roles: You are Dominic now.)

Dominic

4. What • they • do • then?
(That scene was filmed again, and it was OK the second time.)
5. you • able to see • yourself • in new film?
(Yes, the film was shown to us before we left the studio. I liked it!)

8 Passive or not? (→ PB p. 80)

a) *Underline the verb forms in these sentences and write "active" or "passive".*

1. Jane has sent me an invitation to her party!
   active

2. THE ACTORS FOR THE NEW FILM HAVE NOT BEEN CHOSEN YET.
   passive

3. An Internet search engine was used for the first time in 1993.
   passive

b) *Read the sentences, then write what the people say in the speech bubbles. (Decide first: Active or passive?)* (EH)

1. Andy wants to buy a Kyoto Hotel CD, but there aren't any more in the shop.
2. Peter is phoning a friend about his race.
3. Jessica's bike isn't where she left it.

9 Revision: If-clauses (type 2 and 3) (→ PB p. 80)

It's Matt's second week of work at the studio. Change the sentences. Use if-clauses.
Example: Matt is tired in the mornings because he goes to bed late.
→ If he didn't go to bed late, he wouldn't be tired in the mornings.

1. Matt walks to the studio because he doesn't own a car.
   If Matt owned a car, he wouldn't walk to the studio.
2. He forgot his anorak on Monday, so he got very wet on his way to the studio.
   If he hadn't forgotten his anorak, he wouldn't have got wet.
3. The director is angry with Matt because he speaks too quickly.
   If Matt didn't speak too quickly, the director wouldn't be angry with him.
4. Matt didn't meet Kate Winslet at the studio on Thursday because he had gone out to a restaurant.
   If he hadn't gone out to a restaurant, he would have met Kate Winslet at the studio.
5. Matt went to a party yesterday evening, so he didn't have time for football training.
   If Matt hadn't gone to the party, he would have had time for football training.
6. Matt feels happy because he enjoys his work in "EastEnders".
   If he didn't enjoy his work in "EastEnders", he wouldn't feel happy.

TALKWISE

10 Listening: Eric's world (→ PB p. 81) *(Erwartungshorizont S. 89)*

a) *Listen to the story. Copy the grid into your exercise book and make notes.*

Eric's game	"Holo-Comm"	Calm-down[1] belt[2])

b) *Write 1–2 sentences about Eric's home in your exercise book.*

c) *Listen again. Are the sentences right or wrong?*

The sentence is ...	right	wrong
1. Eric is 16 years old.		✔
2. In Eric's world people cannot swim.	✔	
3. Eric eats his meals while he is playing games.		✔
4. Other people's homes are many different colours.		✔
5. In the past there were many more people than there are now.	✔	

d) *Talk to a partner. Would you like to live in Eric's world? Why / Why not?*

11 A role play: Media and the family (→ PB p. 81)

a) *Work in groups of three. Read the two situations on the right and choose one. Decide who is going to play which role. Write dialogues in your exercise books. Your Useful phrases box from ex. 3 on p. 81 in your book can help you.*

b) *Act the dialogues in class.*

A I'd like a new mobile!
3 roles: grandma, grandad, Dennis
Dennis would like to have a new mobile for his birthday. His grandparents think the mobile he has is good enough. Dennis tries to explain how important this type of phone is for a teenager. His grandparents ask a lot of questions ...

B No more Internet games!
3 roles: mum, dad, Amy
Amy's dad got a phone call from her Maths teacher because Amy hasn't done any homework for a week. Her parents are very angry. They tell her that she can't use the Internet any more. Amy tries to tell them why the Internet is important for school ...

12 Your turn: Talk about the media in your life (→ PB p. 81)

a) *Which media are important for you? Which do you like or use most? Copy this grid into your exercise book and make notes about yourself and your media.*

I like ... / use ...	Reasons	I don't like ... / use ...	Reasons

b) *Talk to a partner. Explain why you like some media and don't like others.*

[1] **(to) calm down** [kɑːm ˈdaʊn] = sich beruhigen • [2] **belt** [belt] = Gürtel

13 A commercial for sunglasses (→ PB p. 82)

Put in the past perfect passive.

1. Fashion model Cindy was very happy. She had been chosen (choose) to act in a TV commercial for sunglasses.
2. The sunglasses were very popular. They had been seen (see) in films the year before.
3. Cindy arrived at the studio on Monday. But the day had been changed (change) to Tuesday.
4. Cindy started work on the commercial after her hair had been dyed (dye) black.
5. But her super cool sunglasses were too big. – The wrong size had been ordered (order).
6. Two days later everything was OK. The right sunglasses had been sent (send).
7. But when Cindy saw the commercial on TV, she was shocked. – Her role had been given (give) to a sports star!

14 From football to commercials (→ PB p. 83)

Ron Wayne is a football star. He has just made a TV commercial for pizzas. Write down what has happened to him.
Use the personal passive.

TIP Start with a person, not with a thing!

1. The pizza firm has promised Ron free pizzas for a year.
   Ron has been promised free pizzas for a year (by the pizza firm).
2. Two Italian girls have taught him to speak Italian.
   He has been taught to speak Italian (by two Italian girls).
3. The Casting Director has shown him the best restaurants in town.
   He has been shown the best restaurants in town (by the Casting Director).
4. Young people from his football club have sent him hundreds of fan letters.
   He has been sent hundreds of fan letters (by young people from his football club).
5. Another firm has offered Ron a contract for mobile phone ads.
   Ron has been offered a contract for mobile phone ads (by another firm).
6. His football trainer has given him one week to decide: "Commercials or football?"
   He has been given one week to decide: "Commercials or football?"
   (by his football trainer).

15 A job in a studio: Here's the information (→ PB p. 83)

Teenagers are sometimes cast for small roles in films or commercials. When they arrive for work, Tanya tells them what will happen. What does she say? Use the will future passive.

1. The work will be *explained to you very soon.* — explain • work • very soon
2. *You will be taken to the studio by bus.* — take • to studio • by bus
3. *Your make-up will be checked before we start.* — check • make-up • before • start
4. *You will be taught to dance this afternoon.* — teach • to dance • this afternoon
5. *You will be paid after work.* — pay • after work
6. *People will be cast for new roles on Friday.* — cast • people • new roles • on Friday

16 Mediation: Advertising (→ PB p. 84)

a) *An English friend asks you questions about these German ads. With a partner, ask and answer the questions – in English, of course! Use your exercise book.* ***(Lösungen S. 89)***

1

Keine Power mehr? Hier ist die kleine Mahlzeit für die Pause. Coole Packung, gesunder Inhalt. Viele verschiedene Sorten. Aufmachen und genießen!

2

Nur noch einmal in Deutschland! Bill Robson und Band, live auf der Bühne in Hamburg am 10. Mai. Karten: Online oder bei den Vorverkaufsstellen.

3

Neu eingetroffen! Polohemden in sechs topmodischen Farben. Neue amerikanische Länge. Von Superstar Tommy entworfen.

1. Are they chocolate? What's so good about them? Are they all the same?
2. Is Bill going to be on TV? Will there be more concerts? How can you get tickets?
3. Is that an ad for jeans? Do you get them in other colours then these? What's so special about them?

b) *Read the English ad and answer the questions – in German, of course!*

GLOSS for fantastic hair!
Makes your hair clean, fresh and shiny.
Used by all the top hair stylists and salons.
GLOSS for all hair problems.
Only £3.99 for a big 250 ml bottle.
Special offer for a limited time only:
Buy one bottle, get one FREE!

Was ist "GLOSS"?

Haarwaschmittel.

Was kostet es?

£3.99; zur Zeit gibt es zwei Flaschen für den Preis von einer (Sonderangebot).

Was soll so gut daran sein?

Macht das Haar sauber, frisch und glänzend, löst alle Haarprobleme; von Top-Friseuren und Salons verwendet.

WRITING SKILLS

17 Writing a report (→ PB p. 85)

a) *Choose one of these topics for your report.*

1. An accident in the town centre / on a class trip / …
2. Violence at the football match / at school / …
3. A thief in the supermarket / in the changing rooms / …

Make notes for your report. *(Erwartungshorizont)*

Headline (Choose this at the end.)	*Six cameras stolen in one hour*
Basic information (who, what, when, where)	*girl (15) – stole 6 cameras from department store –* *yesterday afternoon – left store – caught by police outside*
Interesting details (more facts about the basic information)	*girl – seen by assistant – called police –* *her bag and pockets – full of stolen things* *girl – trouble with bullies at school – needed money* *cameras – "ordered" by other thieves*
Background information (about the people, the places, …)	*clever thieves – use teenagers (need money)* *parents / school – don't know* *hundreds of cameras, mobiles, … – stolen every year* *sometimes – sold – Internet*
Useful information (websites, phone numbers, people and places that help)	*Helpline: Stop Bullies!* *Don't buy stolen things! – How to check*

b) *Use your notes from a) and write a report in your exercise book.* *(EH S. 89)*

TIP

- Your **headline** must tell the readers what your report is about – and get them interested!
- Use the **passive** when you don't know who did something (or when you want to say who it was in a "by …" phrase).
- **Don't** give your **opinion** in a report – just write the **facts**!

c) *Work with a partner. Check each other's reports. What advice can you give your partner? (Do you understand everything in the report? Is any information missing? Are some facts or phrases repeated?) The Useful phrases on page 84 in your book can help you.*

18 Bill and Janice (→ PB p. 87)

a) *Read the text. Decide who would say these statements. Write down the name or names.*

1. "Finally you've read one of the library books that I always get for you." Bill's mum
2. "*Harry Potter* made it less boring in hospital." Bill
3. "*ER* isn't that bad after all." Janice's parents
4. "*ER* taught me how to rescue a boy." Janice
5. "The bandage on my leg was really cool!" the boy on the roof

b) *What else would Bill, Janice or their parents say? Write two more statements about the story.* (EH)

Bill: "Books can be fun but only sometimes. When you're ill, for example."

Janice: "TV can sometimes teach you something important for life."

19 Looking at their experiences (→ PB p. 87)

a) *Write down your answers to these questions. (You won't find all the answers in the text.)* (EH)

1. Bill doesn't say why he didn't read books before. Can you think of any reasons?

   It wasn't cool. / His friends didn't read. / He was too busy with other things.

2. What was so good about the Harry Potter book for Bill?

   He could imagine the pictures in his head.

3. Janice could do some useful things for the boy because she had seen them on TV. What were they?

   She climbed up to the roof. / She talked to the "patient" and helped him.

4. Some people say hospital soaps are not realistic. Can you imagine why?

   Every ill person / accident is a drama. / All the doctors are beautiful.

b) *Talk to a partner. Do you think Bill's story and/or Janice's story is funny? Why/Why not?*

20 Writing texts: Imagining the future (→ PB p. 87) (EH S. 89)

The power of the media is growing very quickly today. How are we going to communicate in the future? Will there still be TVs, cinemas, radio shows, the Internet or mobile phones?

Imagine it is the year 2030. How do people use the media now? What is different? Use your ideas in a short story. Write it in your exercise book.

21 Polite conversations (→ PB p. 88) *(Erwartungshorizont)*

Some people are so rude! Change these dialogues and make them polite.

1. Let me help you with that heavy bag.
   – ~~OK, carry it for me.~~ — *Oh, thanks! That's kind of you.*
2. ~~Open the door for me.~~ — *Could you open the door for me, please?*
   – Of course. Just a moment, please.
3. I can't walk any faster. I'm awfully sorry.
   – ~~Come on, hurry up!~~ — *No problem. We aren't in a hurry.*
4. Excuse me, could I ask you a question?
   – ~~What do you want to know?~~ — *Yes, of course. How can I help you?*
5. ~~There isn't any cake for you.~~ — *I'm sorry, but we've finished the cake.*
   – Never mind. Could I have some bread, please?

22 A media puzzle

1. People go to this to listen to live music — 1 C O **N** C E R T
2. This person has files with photos of actors — 2 A G **E** N T
3. A person who reads books all the time — 3 B O O K **W** O R M
4. A place where films and CDs are made — 4 **S** T U D I O
5. A TV drama about people and their problems — 5 S O A **P**
6. An actor signs this when he agrees to play a role — 6 C O N T R **A** C T
7. The text of a film or play — 7 S C R I **P** T
8. A famous person — 8 C **E** L E B
9. A woman who plays roles — 9 A C T **R** E S S
10. Many people buy this and read it every day — 10 NEWSPAPER

23 Word web: Advertising

L	A	I	C	R	E	M	M	O	C	S
E	C	W	P	B	N	A	F	P	C	X
L	E	D	O	M	I	A	N	D	P	H
S	M	U	M	O	L	O	S	E	L	L
U	M	D	K	U	D	W	I	D	S	H
R	A	O	L	B	A	W	O	B	I	Q
E	R	N	Z	T	E	Q	F	U	A	T
T	G	A	T	E	H	F	R	Y	N	T
Q	O	C	A	X	W	Q	A	L	J	R
Z	R	N	P	T	C	U	D	O	R	P
E	P	E	S	I	T	R	E	V	D	A

a) *Find ten advertising words. The letters go up or down, from right to left or from left to right.*

b) *Make a word web with the words from a). Write down the verbs first, then the nouns. Start here:*

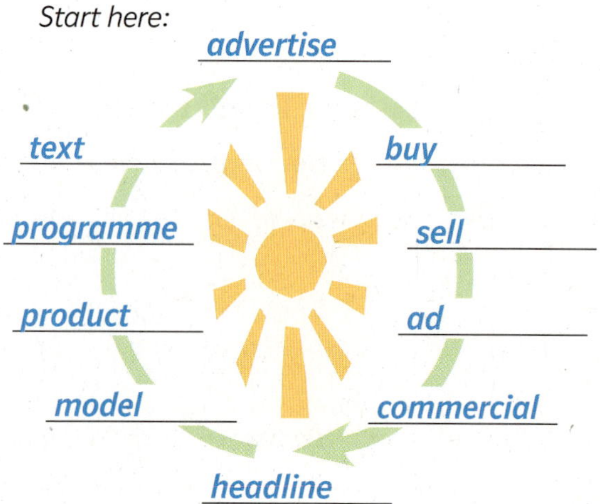

24 New trainers from America (→ PB p. 89)

Complete the sentences with the passive in the correct tense.

Last month SPEED trainers *were advertised* (advertise) on British TV for the first time. Before that they *had not been seen* (not see) in British shops. "300,000 pairs *have been sold* (sell) here this month already!" UK manager Mr Burton said. Two years ago the trainers *were worn* (wear) only by a few top athletes in America. But today they *are bought* (buy) by millions of sports lovers. "Our firm *is known* (know) for its high-quality products," Mr Burton said. "I'm sure lots of races *will be won* (win) with our trainers in Britain, too."

25 Put these sentences into the passive (→ PB p. 89)

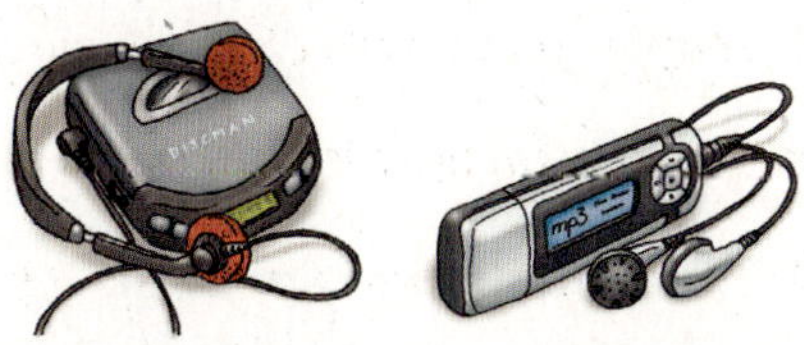

1. In 1984 the Japanese company Sony created the Discman.

   In 1984 the Discman was *created by the Asian company Sony.*

2. Ten years later another company introduced a new music invention.

   Ten years later a new music invention was introduced (by another company).

3. Since then many companies have sold MP3 players to millions of young people.

   Since then MP3 players have been sold to millions of young people (by many companies).

4. Teenagers use them everywhere – even in the bathroom.

   They are used (by teenagers) everywhere – even in the bathroom.

5. Maybe engineers will create a new type of music player in the next few years.

   Maybe a new type of music player will be created (by engineers) in the next few years.

26 Write a report about a class trip (→ PB p. 89)

a) *Choose a topic, then write down notes about the topic.* *(Lösungsvorschlag)*

a match against another school • a visit for a school project • a hike • a trip to a play or concert

When: *last Saturday – after match* Where: *changing rooms*

Who: *our volleyball team – two mice* What happened: *scared; new pets*

b) *Write a short report in your exercise book. Remember to use the passive.* *(EH S. 90)*

c) *Check your partner's report. (Use the Useful phrases on page 84 in your book.)*

⟨Big mouth[1] and ugly[2] girl⟩

At Rocky River High School, Matt Donaghy and Ursula Riggs have little in common[3]. Matt is "big mouth", Ursula is "ugly girl". Then, one day, two detectives walk into the classroom and take Matt away for questioning. He is accused of[4] threatening[5] to blow up the school. Ursula seems to be the only one to see how silly this whole idea is, and she is not afraid to speak out[6]. On the evening of the arrest, she watches the news but doesn't want to talk to her mother about the events.

I'd made Lisa promise not to say anything to Mom about the TV news, and I was surprised – Lisa kept her promise. Or maybe she'd just forgotten? I knew Mom would find out soon, and I didn't want to talk about it with her. While we were eating, I mentioned maybe I'd be quitting the basketball team, and both Lisa and Mom reacted with disappointment. "Oh, Ursula!" Lisa said. "Don't quit, you're so good."

My kid sister's eyes were so beautiful, warm and dark and fine-lashed like a doll's eyes, that sometimes it was hard for Ugly Girl to be jealous of[7] her.

"Ursula! Come here!"

Mom called me downstairs. It was the ten o'clock news. The broadcaster was saying gravely that Rocky River Police were "not yet releasing the identity of a Rocky River High School student who allegedly[8] threatened to bomb the school and massacre hundreds of his classmates and teachers". Cut[9] to a very harassed-looking[10] Mr Parrish backing away from an aggressive reporter shoving a microphone into his face. "I said – I have no comment at this time." Cut to a Rocky River detective. "The alleged incident[11] is being investigated. No, no arrests have been made." Cut to the broadcaster in his studio, with an insert of the façade of Rocky River High in the lower left-hand corner of the screen. "It's believed that a fifteen-year-old student at the high school has been suspended from classes. At the present time it isn't known if the boy has a juvenile record[12] or a psychiatric history or even if he was conspiring[13] with others in the alleged plot[14]. And now – " Cut to Manhattan, the façade of City hall.

"This is so wrong. My God, this is so crazy, and so wrong."

Mom was all agitated[15], as I knew she'd be. Asking if I knew about this. If the school had been "evacuated". I told her it was nothing but a rumour[16]. "Then you know about it, Ursula?"

"No! I mean – I know about the rumour."

"How do you know it's only a rumour?"

Because I was there, I was a witness[17].

I ran my hands through my hair, leaving it spiky. Lisa was still up, in her pyjamas, staring at me wide-eyed. Dad hadn't come home yet. I hoped for Mom's sake that he'd called in, but I didn't remember hearing the phone ring. I started back upstairs, and Mom called after me, "Ursula! What do you know about this? Do you know the boy?"

It was too complicated to get into with Mom. She'd been drinking, I could tell. [...]

I shut the door to my room and locked it. Mom followed me and knocked on the door. "Ursula? What are you doing? Please –" I knew after a few minutes she'd get discouraged[18], if I didn't fall into the trap of exchanging shouts with her through the door.

I was trembling[19], the TV news had made me so angry. Not a bit of it was true – I'd heard exactly what Matt Donaghy had said in the cafeteria, and I'd seen what he'd done. It must be a nightmare[20] for him, I thought.

I wanted to call him but had trouble finding the right Donaghys in the phone book.

adapted from: *Big mouth and ugly girl* by Joyce Carol Oates

[1] **big mouth** ('bɪg maʊθ) = Großmaul • [2] **ugly** ('ʌgli) = hässlich • [3] **(to) have sth in common** (ˌhæv ɪn 'kɒmən) = etw. gemeinsam haben • [4] **(to) be accused of** (bɪ ə'kju:zd‿əv) = unter Anklage stehen • [5] **(to) threaten** ('θretn) = drohen • [6] **(to) speak out** (spi:k 'aʊt) = seine Meinung deutlich vertreten • [7] **(to) be jealous of sb** (bɪ 'dʒeləs‿əv) = auf jmdn. neidisch sein • [8] **allegedly** (ə'ledʒɪdli) = angeblich • [9] **cut** (kʌt) = Schnitt • [10] **harassed-looking** ('hærəstˌlʊkɪŋ) = gestresst aussehend • [11] **incident** ('ɪnsɪdnt) = (Vor)fall • [12] **juvenile record** (ˌdʒu:vnaɪl 'rekɔ:d) = Jugendvorstrafe • [13] **(to) conspire** (kən'spaɪə) = heimlich planen • [14] **plot** (plɒt) = Verschwörung • [15] **agitated** ('ædʒɪteɪtɪd) = aufgeregt, beunruhigt • [16] **rumour** ('ru:mə) = Gerücht • [17] **witness** ('wɪtnəs) = Zeuge, Zeugin • [18] **discouraged** (dɪ'skʌrɪdʒd) = entmutigt • [19] **(to) tremble** ('trembl) = zittern • [20] **nightmare** ('naɪtmeə) = Alptraum

Unit 6 Time to travel

1 Famous journeys (→ PB p. 92) *(Lösungen S. 90)*

a) *Look at the maps. Which map A to D goes with which journey? (You don't need one map.)*

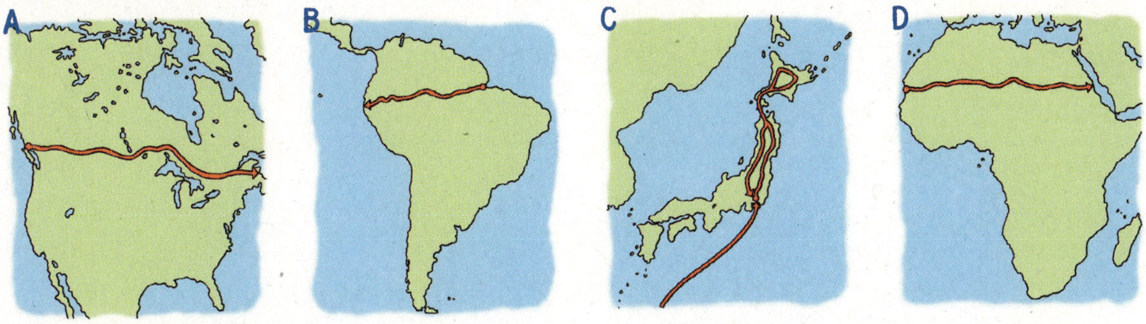

1. Frank Cole was born in Canada. He was very interested in deserts. In 1989 – 1990 he crossed the Sahara alone on a camel. He travelled from the west coast of Africa to the Red Sea in just one year. On his journey it was sometimes very difficult to find enough water. His trip was a success, and he made a beautiful film about it. But when he tried to do the same journey again 10 years later, he was killed by thieves somewhere in the desert.
2. Isabella Bird was born in England. She went on long journeys to Australia, India, Turkey … And that was in the 19th century, when women did not often travel alone. In 1878 she travelled through the north of Japan for some months. She rode on a horse along difficult paths, and she visited people and places which no European had ever seen before. She wrote a book about her journey.
3. In 2005 Kyle Pickering from Canada decided to go on a long walk. He started on the west coast of Canada in January. Soon his friend Bobby McDowell joined him. In summer it was terribly hot, and in winter the temperature was often –30°! Sometimes they saw nobody for days, but on other days they were offered a meal and a bed for the night. After seventeen months the two men arrived at the east coast of Canada. They had walked 7,953 kilometres, and together they had used twenty pairs of shoes.

b) *Copy the grid in your exercise book and make notes about the three travellers in a).* *(EH S. 90)*

Traveller	Region/Country	When?	How long?	How? (Transport)

c) *Which journey would be the scariest for you? Why? Which trip would you like to make? Why? Write in your exercise book.* *(Erwartungshorizont S. 90)*

2 Listening: A trip to Australia (→ PB p 92)

a) *Listen to the discussion. Underline the mistakes in these sentences.*

1. It takes 22 hours to fly from the UK to Australia.
2. It took Captain Cook 3 days to travel to Australia.
3. On Captain Cook's ship there was no fresh air.
4. Ryan is going to Australia next month.

b) *Correct the mistakes and write the sentences in your exercise book.* *(Lösungen S. 90)*

3 "You'll love the beaches!" (→ PB p. 95)

Jade's family is planning a summer holiday. She would love to go to Mallorca. Her best friend Claire thinks it is a really cool place. What does Claire tell Jade about Mallorca? Look at the sentences on the left and write down what Jade tells her parents. Use indirect speech.

direct speech	indirect speech
1. "I'm a great fan of Mallorca!"	Claire told me she was a great fan of Mallorca.
2. "You'll love the beaches and the landscape!"	She said I would love the beaches and the landscape.
3. "We've been to Mallorca three times, and my uncle is planning to buy a flat there."	She said they had been to Mallorca three times and her uncle was planning to buy a flat there.
4. "I took lots of photos of the coast. I'll show them to you.	Claire told me she had taken lots of photos of the coast. She said she would show them to me/us.

4 An e-mail from Australia (→PB p. 95)

a) *Ryan's father sent an e-mail from Australia last week. Read what he said. Underline the time phrases, then make a list and add how they would be reported a few days later.*

Last week the weather was terrible here.
Yesterday it was raining and I couldn't enjoy the day.
And three days ago it was so windy that my hat flew away!
But today the sun is shining.
I really love the ocean, and I'm looking at the water just now.
Tomorrow I'm travelling to Sydney to fly home. So I will see you next week.

Love, Dad

direct speech	indirect speech
last week	the week before
yesterday	the day before
three days ago	three days before
today	that day
just now	just then
tomorrow	the next day
next week	the following week

b) *Ryan tells a friend about his dad's e-mail. How does he report what his father wrote? Write in your exercise book. You can start: Dad said that the weather had been …* **(Lösungen S. 90)**

5 Three very different trips (→ PB p. 95)

Read the reports. Write down what they actually said. (You can underline the verb forms first.)

1. Tanya said she had gone to Canada for six months the year before. The winters were always cold there, but she had never had cold feet on her trip. She was going to go back there the following year.

   "I went to Canada for six months last year. The winters are always cold there, but I never had cold feet on my trip. I'm going to go back there next year."

2. Jonas said he had just come back from a trip to India. He would never forget his first trip on an elephant. The following day he had wanted to fly over the high mountains, but the weather had not been good enough.

   "I've just come back from a trip to India. I'll never forget my first trip on an elephant! The next day I wanted to fly over the high mountains, but the weather wasn't good enough."

3. Jessica said that five days before she had begun her boat trip on a big lake in Italy. She did not know what had happened then, but the day before she had woken up in hospital. She was staying there until the following week, because she had broken her foot.

   "Five days ago I began my boat trip on a big lake in Italy. I don't know what happened then, but yesterday I woke up in hospital. I'm staying here until next week, because I've broken my foot."

6 Mediation: What about a holiday in Sydney? *(Lösungen S. 90)*

Olli Möller would like to go to Sydney. His family are asking him about this website. Talk to a partner. How does Olli answer the questions (in German)?

Come to Sydney, the largest city in Australia! Everybody knows the city's world famous landmark – the Opera House. On our guided tour you can find out fascinating facts, listen to cool music – and climb 200 steps!
Then there's Sydney Harbour Bridge. For really adventurous people we offer a three-hour guided tour right to the top of the bridge! Enjoy the fantastic view of the harbour – and get a certificate, too! But it's definitely not a trip for nervous people! Why not see the harbour from the water? That's really relaxing. Our water taxis take you where you want to go. No noise, no crowds.
If you like action, crowds and fun – try Luna Park. There are rides and shows for the whole family – ferris wheel, pirate ship, souvenirs, snacks …
Last but not least, we've got 30 beaches where you can learn to surf or go scuba diving. You can swim in the warm water all year round, or just enjoy the sun. (But don't forget that sun hat!)

Frau M: Eine Großstadt! Das ist bestimmt furchtbar unruhig! Wie soll ich mich dort erholen?
Sven (12 J.): Das klingt ganz schön langweilig. Gibt es nichts, was Jugendlichen Spaß macht?
Herr M: Wenn ich um die halbe Welt fliegen muss, will ich etwas Einmaliges erleben. Was hast du über die berühmte Brücke herausgefunden?
Melanie (16 J.) Ich will baden und braun werden. Das geht doch auch in Sydney, oder?

TALKWISE

7 Books, films and computer games (→ PB p. 96)

a) *Read the texts about these books, games and films. Then guess the kind of book, film or game and tick ✔ the right box.*

1 When we watched *Ever Popular*, we laughed all the time. The story was about this young teenage celebrity. She wore the hottest clothes and she was really funny too. You'd love it!

2 *Alien Battle* is disappointing. I played for 5 minutes and got bored. It's not scary or exciting, so I'm happy I borrowed it. And it's quite expensive, too. I really wouldn't recommend it.

3 *Planet Wars* is on at the theatre now. It all happens in the future in a world called Ouros with aliens that are at war. There are some very exciting scenes too. You'd enjoy this a lot!

4 *All about Marco* is the true story about the life of the Italian Marco Polo. It is brilliant and filled with adventure. He is a really famous traveller. If you want my advice, read this story now!

1. *Ever Popular* is
   a) a comedy. ☑ b) a science fiction game. ☐ c) an action film. ☐
2. *Alien Battle* is
   a) an action film. ☐ b) a battle game. ☑ c) a science fiction story. ☐
3. *Planet Wars* is
   a) a thriller. ☐ b) a battle game. ☐ c) a science fiction film. ☑
4. *All about Marco* is
   a) a thriller ☐ b) a love story ☐ c) a biography. ☑

b) *Choose one of your favourite books, films or games. Make notes about it.*

What kind? Characters? What happens? Good points?

1. *Tell your partner about it. Then listen to your partner's report about his/her game, book or film.*
2. *Ask your partner questions. Look at the tips on page 96 in your book first.*

8 Guess the title! (→ PB p. 96)

Play this game with a partner. Take turns. First your partner thinks of a popular film, book or computer game. You must try to find out the title. Before you start, choose the rules for your game:

a) *You can ask questions, but your partner may only answer with yes or no. You have twenty questions.*

You	Your partner
1. Is it a film?	– Yes, it is.
2. Is it a science fiction film?	– No, it isn't.
3. Is it an action film?	– Yes, it is.
4. … ?	– …

b) *Your partner's answers must not be longer than three words. You have ten questions. (But you can't ask: What's the title?)*

You	Your partner
1. Is it a book, a film or a game?	– A book.
2. What kind of book is it?	– A love story.
3. … ?	– …

9 Reporting in the present (→ PB p. 97)

a) *Read the statements on the left. Then draw a line to the verbs which are best to report them.*

1. Police Officer:	You have to leave the area because of the fire.	ask
2. Ryan:	What's happened?	explain
3. Police Officer:	There has been a fire in the Webbs' house.	suggest
4. Police Officer:	Please move now! Or you'll get hurt.	advise
5. Police Officer:	You can find out more in the newspaper later.	warn

b) *Now use the present tense of the verbs you chose in a) to put the statements into indirect speech. Watch out! Sometimes you need to use the infinitive to report what was said. Use your exercise book. Start like this:* 1. The police officer advises Ryan … *(Lösungen S. 90)*

10 Tandem activity: At the audition (→ PB p. 98)

TIP
Use 'if' or 'whether' when you report a question without a question word.

Amy and Linda have just been to auditions – but not together. Now they are talking on the phone. First Amy asks questions and Linda reports what the director said. Then Amy asks questions and Linda reports.

Amy

1. director • ask • first?
   (He asked me why I wanted to be in the show.)
2. he • talk • music?
   (Yes, he asked what my favourite music was.)
3. he • ask • anything else?
   (Yes, he wanted to know if I enjoyed auditions.)
4. you • ask • questions?
   (Yes, I asked him when the rehearsals would start.)
5. (What questions did the director ask you?)
   "Have you ever done a casting?"
6. (Did he ask about music?)
   "Where did you learn to dance?"
7. (Did you ask him any questions?)
   "Do you make commercials here?"
8. (Was that your only question?)
   "How much will I earn?"

Linda

1. (What did the director ask you first?)
   "Why do you want to be in the show?"
2. (Did he talk about music?)
   "What's your favourite music?"
3. (Did he ask you anything else?)
   "Do you enjoy auditions?"
4. (Did you ask him any questions?)
   "When will the rehearsals start?"
5. what • questions • director • ask?
   (He asked me whether I had ever done a casting.)
6. he • ask • music?
   (No, but he asked me where I had learned to dance.)
7. you • ask • questions?
   (Yes, I asked if he made commercials there.)
8. your • only question?
   (No, I asked him how much I would earn.)

11 What the director said (→ PB p. 98) *(Lösungen S. 90)*

In your exercise book write down what the director said to the girls. Use indirect commands. Start with: The director told them …

1. "Speak a bit more clearly, please."
2. "Tell me about your dancing lessons."
3. "Don't sit on the cold floor!"
4. "Imagine you're princesses in a palace."
5. "Please don't phone me every day next week!"

12 Listening: An accident in Upton Road (→ PB p. 99)

Listen an fill out the form for the operator. Write down information or put an X in the box.

✚ STOCKWOOD EMERGENCY SERVICES ✚

Caller:	**Name:**	Mr *X* Mrs ☐ *Watts*
	Address:	Road: *Upton Road* Number: *10*
	Service:	Police ☐ Ambulance *X* Fire ☐
Accident:	**Place:**	*Upton Road*
	Reason:	Traffic ☐ Attack / Fight ☐ Fall *X* Other ☐
	Person hurt:	Man ☐ Woman ☐ Child *X*
	**Part of body hurt:**	Head *X* Leg Arm ☐ Back ☐ Other ☐
	Details:	Broken ☐ Trapped ☐ Bleeding *X* Other ☐

13 How to: Make an emergency call (→ PB p. 99)

a) *Think of a situation for an emergency call. Make notes in your exercise book about what has happened.*

thief has broken into factory • tree has fallen on house • fire has started in farm building • …

b) *Act out the dialogue with a partner. Use the Useful phrases on page 99 in your book.*

c) *Write the dialogue in your exercise book.* *(Erwartungshorizont S. 90)*

14 Revision: Questions with prepositions (→ PB p. 99) *(EH)*

Some younger brothers want to know everything!
What does Max ask his sister Rachel?
Find your own funny answers.

think about • wait for • bark at • fight over • talk to ✓

1. *Who are you talking to?* – *I'm talking to Robbie Williams.*
2. *What are you waiting for?* – *I'm waiting for a call from my manager.*
3. *Who / What is the dog barking at?* – *He's barking at a tiger in the tree.*
4. *What are you fighting over?* – *We're fighting over a photo of you!*
5. *What are you thinking about?* – *I'm thinking about my most important secret.*

SPEAKING SKILLS

15 Small talk (→ PB p. 100)

A Show that you are listening

The speakers are in a café in the USA. How do they show they are listening to what the other person says? Complete the dialogue with phrases from the box below.

Exactly. | Oh, I see. | Really? | Yes, I know. | Oh no! | Right.

A: Hello. Is it OK if I sit here?

B: Yes, sure. A guy was sitting there, but he's gone now.

A: ***Oh, I see.*** This café is always full. It's very popular.

B: ***Yes, I know.*** The food is very good, and the view is fantastic. Film stars often come here.

A: ***Really?*** I must keep my eyes open! Now, what can I order? Last week I had a salad in town, and there was a spider in it!

B: ***Oh no!*** Why don't you have a curry today? The fish curry here is very good. I can really recommend it.

A: ***Right.*** I'll try that. I think you should eat food that you don't get at home.

B: ***Exactly.*** Oh, look. The waitress is coming to our table now.

B Continue the conversation *(Erwartungshorizont)*

You are on a long bus journey in Canada. The passenger next to you says something to you, and you would like to continue the conversation. How could you reply to these sentences?

1. We'll be in Montreal in about an hour. – ***Oh good! I've never been there before.***
2. I always get hungry when I'm travelling. – ***I have some sweets here. Would you like one?***
3. Bus journeys are so boring, aren't they? – ***Yes, they are. I like planes and trains better.***
4. It must be very windy outside. – ***Yes, you're right. Just look at those trees!***

16 A cartoon (→ PB p. 100)

a) *What is happening/has happened in the cartoon?*
Work with a partner. Do you think it is funny? Why/why not?

b) *Choose one of the following tasks:*
How do you think the conversation between the two men might continue? Act it out as a role play with your partner.
or:
Think of a funny small talk situation and act it out as a role play with your partner.

"I just said how are you – I dind't think you'd get on the bus to tell me.""

17 Looking at the story (→ PB p. 103) *(Erwartungshorizont)*

a) *Divide the story "My big adventure" into four different parts. Look for changes in time ("… on the third day…"), in place ("After Nevada …"), in luck or events ("I was wrong!"). Write down the line numbers of the parts.*

A: line 9 – line *22* B: *line 22–48* C: *line 49–89* D: *line 90* – 123

b) *What happens in the different parts? Write one sentence for each part. (Use the present tense!)*

A: *The train journey starts, and the girl meets Phileas Fogg and his friends.*

B: *Thousands of buffalo cross the track and the train must wait until they have gone.*

C: *A dangerous bridge breaks after the train has crossed it.*

D: *Hundreds of Sioux attack the train, and there is a terrible fight.*

c) *Find a good heading for each part.*

A: *Three interesting passengers*

B: *Problems with buffalo*

C: *A difficult decision*

D: *A gun battle with the Sioux*

18 Imagine you are a Sioux (→ PB p. 103) *(Erwartungshorizont)*

Work with a partner. Imagine you are one of the Sioux in the story. Write what you think about the people. Are you happy they are fighting? Are you sad? Write three sentences.

1. *If the white people don't hurt us, we'll leave them alone.*
2. *But this is our land, and many white people want to take it.*
3. *They come here and kill our people and animals, so they must die, too.*

19 Writing texts: Write a group story (→ PB p. 103) *(Erwartungshorizont S. 90)*

a) *Work in a group. Take turns to write the rest of this story. Write one sentence, then give the piece of paper to the next person. Go on like this until you have finished. Here is the beginning of the story.*

One day an Australian student called Brad fell asleep at his desk and had the strangest dream. It was the year 1875, and Brad was on a sailing ship on his way to Australia. The weather was bad, and many passengers felt sick. Brad tried to help one man who was very ill, but nobody could save him. Just before the man died, he gave Brad a small box and told him it would help him when he was in danger. Two days later the captain suddenly shouted, "Pirate ship!" …

b) *Read the story in your group. Think of how you can improve the story and make it more exciting.*

20 A crossword

Across: →
3. If you like a film or book, you … it to your friends
7. A kind of food which comes from Asia
8. A big bus
13. A person who travels
14. A … is a person who helps when there is a fire

Down: ↓
1. "Leave here now!" is a …
2. A long trip
4. You see it at night in the sky
5. We do this when a person comes back from a trip
6. A person who works with ambulances
9. A bad person who steals from houses
10. Use these to stop your car
11. We put them in our gardens
12. If a film or show is not exciting you get …

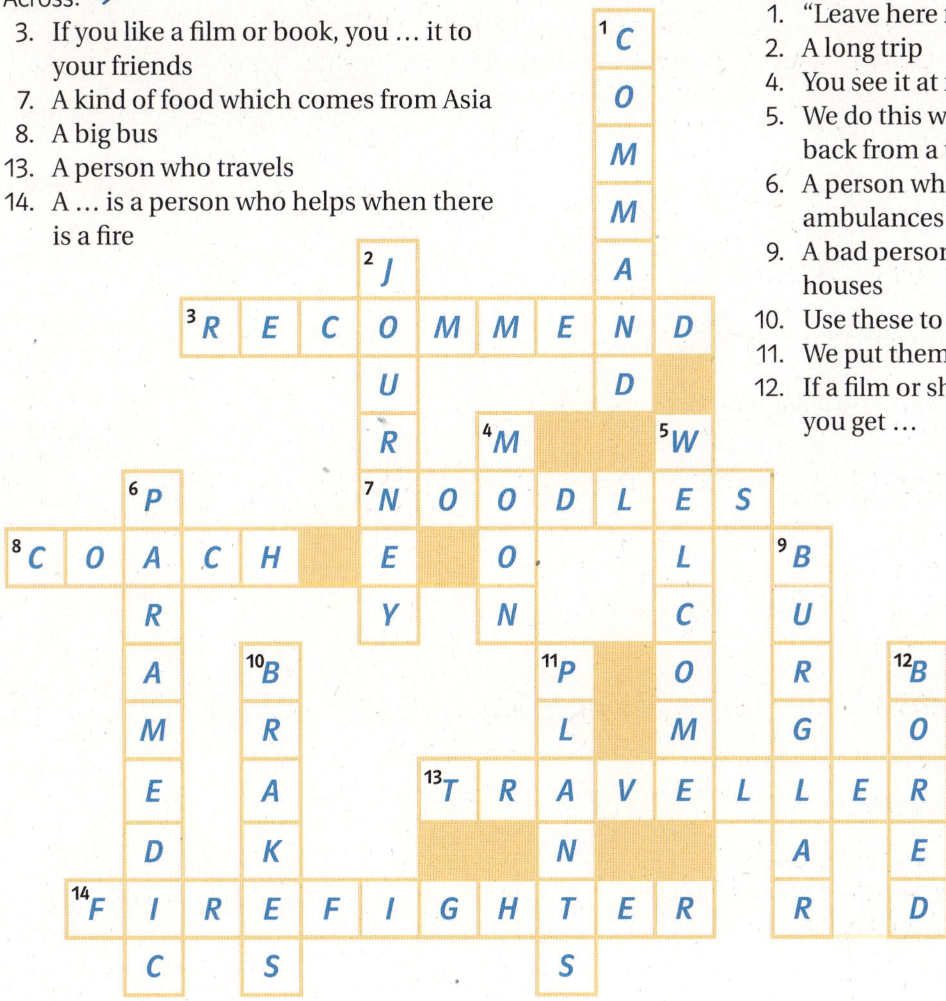

21 Sounds and spelling (→ PB p. 104)

You say the same pair of letters differently in one of the words. Underline that word.

1. [e] leap • seat • scream • dead
2. [aʊ] below • slow • down • own
3. [ɜː] journey • Sioux • through
4. [ʊ] moon • look • noodle • soon

22 Prepositions (→ PB p. 104)

Complete these sentences with the correct preposition.

1. The railway was completed ___in___ 1869.
2. We left the station ___at___ six o'clock in the evening.
3. We travelled ___over___ great prairies.
4. I almost jumped ___out___ of my skin.
5. The train driver was not ready to give up ___up___ easily.
6. Did the other people ___on___ the train survive?

23 Indirect Speech: Can that be right? (→ PB p. 105)

We know that people sometimes say one thing one day – and another thing the next. Ryan's father often does that! He's back home with his family now. Finish Ryan's sentences.

1. "We're going to spend our next holiday in the USA."

   But you said *we were going to spend our next holiday in Australia!* — Australia

2. "My friend Jim learned to play rugby in Australia."

   But you told me he had learned to play golf! — golf

3. "All the Australians watch drama on TV."

   But you said they all watched sports! — sports

4. "Mum has booked a flight to New York."

   But you told me she had booked a flight to Sydney! — Sydney

24 Group Competition: What have you learnt in Green Line 3? (→ PB p. 105)

a) *Work in groups. Write down the answers. (You can find all of them in your book.)*

1. Athletics is an important part of the … *O L Y M P I C G A M E S*
2. Queen … spent more than 63 years on the throne. *V I C T O R I A*
3. Shakespeare's theatre in London is called the … *G L O B E T H E A T R E*
4. A big TV event on American Football. *S U P E R B O W L*
5. Francis … was a British sea captain who fought for Elizabeth I. *D R A K E*
6. Britain is part of the European … *U N I O N*
7. This company made the first colour TV in 1954. *R C A*
8. The wings for the European … plane come from North Wales. *A I R B U S*
9. A popular British soap opera. *E A S T E N D E R S*
10. The language of the Internet. *H T M L*
11. Liverpool is on the river … *M E R S E Y*
12. The reign of Queen Victoria is the age of the British … *E M P I R E*

b) *Write the first letters of your answers in a) in the same order as the sentence numbers. Which group can finish first?*

H	A	V	E	A	G	O	O	D	S	U	M	M	E	R	!
10	8	2	12	8	3	1	1	5	4	6	11	11	9	7	

⟨Revision for Tests⟩ Unit 5–6

1 Mixed bag

a) *Complete the passive sentences.*

Debbie, Tom and Anne *have been* invited to a casting for Coronation Street. They are at the studio now. Their photos *were* sent to the Casting Director a few days ago. After they *had been* told about the casting, they started to learn their 'sides'. The script for the casting *is* called the 'sides'. A photo *has been* taken of them. Their comments about the casting *are* given below.

b) *Read Debbie's, Tom's and Anne's comments and write down what they say or said. Look at the tense of the reporting verb. Use your exercise book. Start like this:* Debbie said she … ***(Lösungen S. 90)***

Debbie: "I was very nervous before the interview yesterday, but I'm fine this evening."
Tom: "The Casting Director is checking my script, because she wants me to play the role differently."
Anne: "I'm really super-happy! I've been chosen to act the role of Tracey."

2 Writing a newspaper report

a) *Complete the tips for writing a newspaper report. Look at page 85 in your book again.*

Tips for writing a newspaper report	Notes
1. Think of a good *headline* (when you have finished the article).	*Britain's must-see places*
2. Give the *basic information* (who, what, when, where) in the first paragraph.	press conference last Monday; Lonely Planet's list of must-see places this year; Cornwall only place in Britain in list
3. Add *interesting details*.	reasons given by Lonely Planet: fantastic coast, beautiful landscape, region's history + culture
4. Give some *background information* on the topic in another paragraph.	survey of tourists done last year; fresh farm food + fish used in pubs; good swimming + surfing in Atlantic; open-air theatre + concerts; shops with traditional arts + crafts; walks along coast paths
5. Finish with *useful information*.	for tourist information: www.visitcornwall.co.uk for surf news: www.magicseaweed.com
6. Use the *passive* when you don't know who did the action or if it's not important.	
7. Don't give your *opinion* in a newspaper report.	

b) *Look at the notes in a) and write the article. Think of a headline after you have finished.* ***(EH S. 91)***

3 How to: Get help in an emergency *(Erwartungshorizont S. 91)*

a) *Look at the three pictures and answer these questions:*
Which service do you need? Where are you calling from? What has happened? Make notes about the important facts in your exercise book.

1

2

3

b) *Compare your notes with a partner.*
Write short dialogues. The Useful phrases on page 99 in your book can help you.
Use your own ideas, too.

c) *Practise the emergency calls with your partner.*
Speak clearly – and stay calm! Your partner can ask more questions.

4 An unexpected birthday present *(Erwartungshorizont S. 91)*

a) ***Before you read:*** *Talk to a partner. What do you like more – playing computer games or reading? Think of an idea for a new computer game or a story.*

It was Simon's 13th birthday and he had been given the last of the Harry Potter books, 'Harry Potter and the Deathly Hallows'. He was happy about that. He liked books. He was good at English, but Maths was a problem for him – and there was a Maths test the next week. He felt very bad about it. Never mind. There would be time to worry about that later. Today was his birthday.

He had been given some other presents, too. One of them was a computer game. It was called 'School Tricks'. "How boring," he thought to himself, but later he went up to his room to try it out anyway.

The sound of the new Arctic Monkeys' single was coming from his sister's bedroom. He opened the box and slowly put the CD into his computer, but a warning suddenly flashed up on the screen: NOT FOR TEACHERS OR PARENTS! He had to register the game online. He was not sure what to expect, but as soon as he opened the menu he knew that this game was something special. He clicked on 'Next weeks' lessons', … 'Wednesday' … 'Maths'. He was getting very excited and could feel the sweat on his hands. He was lost in his new game. No, it wasn't a game. It was more than that.

The smell of food came up to his room from the kitchen below. He had been hungry, but that was forgotten now. His mother called him, but he didn't hear her. He moved the mouse. Fast, then faster. Mr Jackson, his Maths teacher, was holding the test papers. He clicked on them. "Wow!" he cried …

b) ***After you have read the story:*** *Look at exercise 5a)/b) on page 103 in your book again. How does the author try to make this story more interesting? Find examples.*

c) ***Writing texts:*** *Choose one of these activities.*
1. *Continue the story.*
2. *Describe Simon's game for a computer game magazine.*
3. *Write an advertisement for the game. Look at exercise 6 on page 84 in your book again.*

VOCABULARY SKILLS

You use words when you speak, write, read or listen. So if you improve your vocabulary skills, it will help you to improve all your other language skills, too! Try to learn a few new words every day.

1 Use different ways to guess new words

TIP

1 Some words are almost the same as German.
2 Latin or French can sometimes help.
3 Maybe you know a word from the same word family.
4 The context often makes the meaning clear.

a) *Guess the meaning of the red words on the right. Make a grid in your exercise book with the English and German words and the tip(s) that helped you.* ***(EH S. 91)***

b) *Compare grids with a partner. Did you think of the same German words? Did you use the same tips?*

The Horse of the Year Show in Birmingham is the highlight of the British **equestrian calendar**. More than 150,000 **competitors** try to **qualify** for the show at events around the country, but in the end only 150 **riders** get to the big **arena** in Birmingham. Every year 55,000 **spectators** watch the competitions; 1,500 horses **take part**; together the horses jump over 8,640 **fences**; workers at the show must collect and take away 220 **tons** of horse **manure**!

2 Word groups

a) *Write down a verb for all the nouns.*

1. *make* : friends • a mistake • money
2. *have* : success • fun • breakfast
3. *take* : a risk • turns • a photo
4. *do* : a trick • sport • your best

b) *Underline the wrong noun for the adjective.*

1. heavy: bag • accident • rain • traffic
2. tall: athlete • building • tree • jump
3. easy: trick • match • racket • question
4. happy: fan • birthday • number • end

3 Get help from a dictionary *(Lösungen S. 91)*

TIP

A dictionary tells you how you can use a word (verb, noun, adjective etc.)

a) *Look up 'track' in an English-German dictionary. Check the meaning in different contexts. Then put these sentences into German. Write in your exercise book.*

1. There will be a new track for the Olympic Games.
2. The train hit something on the track.
3. TV cameras track the ball for the whole match.
4. The hikers followed the track into the hills.
5. The reporter tracked down the star in her hotel.
6. I often lose track of time on the phone.

b) *Now look up 'field'. Make your own sentences with the different meanings as a noun and a verb.*

c) *Use a German-English dictionary to help you put these phrases into English. (Look up the verbs.)*

1. Das macht nichts. – *That doesn't matter.*
2. Das geht doch nicht! – *You can't do that!*
3. Danke, das reicht. – *Thanks, that's enough.*
4. Ich hab's geschafft! – *I did it!*
5. Das gibt's doch nicht! – *That can't be true!*
6. Lass mal sehen. – *Let's have a look.*

d) *When might you use the phrases in c)? With a partner, write and act little dialogues.*

READING SKILLS

Historical texts can be about events, famous people, life in the past etc. You need to read a text more than once. Different reading skills help you first to find your way into the the text and then to learn more about the subject.

TIP

- Don't expect to understand everything right away.
- First read the whole text quickly.
- Then read it again slowly, one part after another.
- Underline important information, or take notes.

1 Think before you read *(EH S. 92)*

On a history tour of the city of Coventry you see the woman in the photo. What do you want to know about her? Write five questions in your exercise book. (When?/Why?/…).

2 Read the text on the right for gist

Match the headings with the five paragraphs of the text. Show the order with the numbers 1 to 5.

Godiva wants to help: 3 Not always all true: 1 Time for action: 4 Not clever to be curious: 5 A hard life under Leofric: 2

3 Read again for detail *(EH S. 92)*

a) *Underline all the words and phrases that tell you about Godiva.*

b) *Look at your questions from exercise 1. Use the information you underlined in the text to answer as many of the questions as you can. Write your answers in your exercise book.*

c) *Take notes about Leofric to show his character* ***before*** *and* ***after*** *Godiva's action. Use your exercise book.*

4 Think about what you have read

a) *Talk about why some details about Godiva may not be true, even in the earliest reports. What can you say about the character Tom?*

b) *Collect ideas about how we can find out about the past. How will people in the future know about events that are happening today?*

It is not always easy to be sure about events that happened hundreds of years ago. In historical stories, facts are sometimes mixed with interesting or exciting details which may not be true. An example of this is the story of Lady Godiva of Coventry.

Lady Godiva was a real person who lived in the early part of the eleventh century, before the Normans arrived in England. She was married to Leofric, a rich and important lord. In those days a lord was able to make his own rules for the people on his land. It was unlucky for the people of Coventry that they lived on Leofric's land. He was a hard man who took money from everyone, even from the poorest families. He was also very strict with the Church. Priests were not allowed to say anything against him.

Because Godiva was a religious woman, she worried about Leofric's problems with the Church. It also made her very sad to see how horrible he was to the people of Coventry. A kind and gentle person, she told Leofric he should be fair to the people. She told him this again and again. Finally Leofric got fed up and said "I'll do what you want if you ride without any clothes through the town on market day!"

Leofric thought his words were no risk for him. He did not believe his shy wife was the kind of woman who could ever do what he had said. He was wrong! Godiva wanted to help the people so much that she rode through Coventry without any clothes. Nobody saw her body because her long hair hid it. After that Leofric became a much kinder person. He was fair to the people, and even gave money to the Church.

The two earliest reports we have of these events are from the twelfth and thirteenth centuries, and that is how the story is told in them. Maybe even then, a long time after Godiva had died in 1067, not all the details were correct. A later report from the seventeenth century brought a new character, Tom, into the story. In this report, the people of Coventry promised not to watch Godiva while she rode through the town. Only Tom looked at her, and from that moment he was never able to see anything again!

LISTENING SKILLS

It is important to understand what you hear if someone is giving you information or if you are having a conversation. Listen to English as often as you can. Songs are good for your listening skills, too!

1 Listening: Listen for keywords

When you phone for information, you often have to choose what you listen to. Read what these people think before they phone the cinema. Then listen and write down the correct numbers.

TIP
Get ready before you phone or ask someone for information. Think about what you want to know.

1. I wonder what they're showing this week. Number 2
2. Hm. Will the café still be open after the late film? Number 7
3. I don't know that cinema. What about my wheelchair? Number 4
4. It'll be a popular film, so it's best if I buy a ticket now. Number 1
5. Right, I've decided! I'll join the Film Club. Number 5

2 Listening: Take notes while you listen

a) *You are going to hear some tips on the radio about things you can do next weekend. Don't worry if you don't understand every word. Just listen for the important information and take notes. Start a new box for every tip.*

TIP
Short forms of words can help you to write more quickly:
Sat = Saturday; St = street;
am = in the morning; + = and; …

drama workshop – ages 11–16 – Sat – Royal Theatre – 9 am–6 pm – £10

Italian Kitchen – Victoria St – 2 pizzas for price of 1 – Sat + Sun – until 3 pm

Technology Museum – free – open every day 10 am–5 pm – Sun 2 pm–5.30 pm

ghost tour – starts outside tourist info office – 6.30 pm – £6.50

b) *Work with a partner. First check if you wrote down the same information. Then choose one thing you want to do together, and make arrangements about when and where to meet.*

3 Listening: Listen carefully to the sounds of words

a) *Listen to two phone calls and read the notes. Cross out and correct the mistake in each note.*

b) *Talk about why you think the mistakes happened. What problems might there be for Ed and Lisa?*

c) *Listen and draw a circle round the word you hear.*

1. A **van/fan** hit an actor in the street.
2. It's a very good **price/prize**, isn't it?
3. The woman had a problem with her **bag/back**.
4. I think small **glasses/classes** are better.
5. He'll be **fifteen/fifty** on his next birthday.
6. The two boys never **thought/fought** about girls.

Message for Ed
Tom called – has got ~~free~~ tickets for football match on Saturday – if you want one, phone back this evening.

Lisa
message from Kelly – boyfriend having party tomorrow – ~~14~~, Field Way – starts 7.30

READING SKILLS

There are so many factual texts on every subject that you cannot read them all! Reading skills can help you to choose the texts that are useful for you and to get the information you want from them.

1 Pre-reading (Erwartungshorizont)

The text at the bottom of this page is part of a brochure about Lincolnshire, a region of England. Use the heading and the photo to write down what you think the text is about.

I think the text is about food from the region.

TIP
While you skim, underline keywords that show what the text is about.

2 Skim the text for the gist

Look through the text quickly. Then read these sentences and write 'true' or 'false'.

1. Lincolnshire has lots of big cities. *false*
2. There are different kinds of farms. *true*
3. Part of the region is next to the sea. *true*
4. People there are not interested in food. *false*

3 Scan the text for information

a) *Look for the answers to these quiz questions. Write the answers in your exercise book.* *(Lösungen S. 92)*

1. Where is Lincolnshire?
2. What grows in the Fens? (2 things)
3. What does the name 'the Wolds' mean?
4. What kind of food is Grimsby famous for?
5. How many towns have Farmers Markets?
6. What tells you there is regional food on the menu?

b) *Find these new words in the text. Use your vocabulary skills to guess the meaning. Then check your own answers with a dictionary.*

1. forest • 2. soil • 3. dairy product • 4. top quality • 5. windmill • 6. port

TIP
Use texts you read to collect useful new words.

4 Read and collect more information

Look on the Internet for more information about Lincolnshire. The ideas on the right can help you to start. Everyone chooses a different idea and tells the group what they find out.

Lincoln
Skegness
the Humber
Gibraltar Point
Donna Nook

TASTES OF LINCOLNSHIRE

Lincolnshire, in the east of England, does not have mountains, great forests or many large cities, but it is a region with its own special character: big skies, wonderful churches, friendly market towns, and some of the best farmland! The part of the region called the Fens is only just above sea level, and many of the country's finest vegetables grow in the rich soil there. Between the vegetables there are fields of beautiful flowers. Further north, the Wolds (the name means 'open land') are home to the cows and sheep whose milk helps to make tasty dairy products like handmade cheese, ice-cream and yoghurt. Lincolnshire farms also produce top quality meat, while many of the old windmills still make flour which bakers use for bread and cakes. Fish plays an important role in the region, too. More fish arrives in the port of Grimsby than in any other port on the coast of Britain. It is no surprise that Lincolnshire people feel strongly about good food and are proud of their traditions. Although a lot goes to other parts of the country, not everything is allowed to leave! Thirteen towns have regular Farmers Markets where people can buy directly from the farmers. Many hotels and restaurants also cook traditional recipes with local food. Visitors should look for the 'Tastes of Lincolnshire' sign on the menu. Then they can be sure they will have the chance to enjoy the best of the region!

WRITING SKILLS

Reports tell readers about news stories, interesting events, special situations etc. With good writing skills you can write reports clearly, in the correct style, and with correct grammar and spelling.

1 Give information in a good order *(EH)*

These notes for a report are in the wrong order. Choose a good order and complete the grid with the letters.

Order	1	2	3	4	5	6
Notes	D	C	F	A	B	E

A
hard job • for Grace Adams, 16, a wet job, too • "I got a broken skateboard and an old shoe out of the lake!"

B
after many hours • park clean again • young workers tired • proud of their work • had made a real difference

C
more than 20 girls and boys • worked all day • lots of rubbish everywhere • had been left on paths • on the grass

D
Victoria Park • looks great • thanks to HI5 Youth Club • last Saturday • big group • met in park • collected all the rubbish

E
teenagers • hope • in future • people • look after the park • Harry Nelson, 15: "Please take your rubbish home with you!"

F
all kinds of rubbish • paper • glass • everything sorted • put into different bags • taken away for recycling

2 Use good writing style *(EH S. 92)*

Use the notes in exercise 1 to write a report in your exercise book. Work in the order you chose, and turn the notes into sentences. The tips can help you. Think of a good headline for the report.

TIP

Use paragraphs for different parts of a report.
- Link ideas with connecting words: and/but/because/after/…
- Put in phrases of time: first/then/…
- Adjectives and adverbs make any text more interesting.
- Don't repeat the same words too often.

3 Correct and improve your own work

a) *With a partner, make a list of things you should think about when you check your own texts.*
b) *Use your list from a) to correct and improve your own report.*

- past forms
- articles (a/the)
- spelling • …

4 Practise your writing skills *(Erwartungshorizont S. 92)*

a) *You are going to write a new report about some young people who took action to raise money. First look at these three events. Choose one that you would like to write about in your report.*

1. Group of teenagers play music in city centre.
2. Group of teenagers organise bike ride.
3. Group of students organise cake sale.

b) *Work with the event you chose in a). Think of information for your report. Don't worry about the order yet. Just collect ideas in a word web. Ask yourself: Who? Where? When? Why? What? …?*

c) *Now plan your report. Put the ideas in your word web into a good order and write notes.*

d) *Use your notes to write your report. Think about style and find a good headline.*

e) *Exchange reports with a partner and help each other to improve your work.*

TIP

- Start a report with a few basic facts.
- Then describe events in more detail.
- Sometimes you need to give background information about a topic.
- Think of a good way to end the report.
- The headline should make the topic clear.

PROJECT SKILLS

When you do a project, you have to work in a group, plan the project, find information, and then prepare and give an interesting presentation. This takes lots of different skills! Practise here with a project on a Commonwealth country.

1 Make groups and choose your topic

Think who you can work well with, and make groups of four or five. Choose a Commonwealth country you are all interested in. Look at the map at the back of your book.

TIP
- Give everyone in the group a chance to speak.
- Listen to other people's ideas.
- If you can't agree, vote to make decisions.

2 Plan your project

Collect ideas for your project and write them down on a big piece of paper. Then plan the work.

basic facts? • climate? • people and traditions? • music? • sports? • interesting animals?

TIP
- Make a list of all the jobs.
- Decide who is going to do what.
- Write down when things must be ready.
- Give everyone a copy of the plan.

3 Get information

a) *First remind yourself how to work with texts. Draw lines to the correct endings of these tips.*

1. Skimming helps you to	find the information you are looking for.
2. Scanning helps you to	write down phrases with the main ideas.
3. Only use a dictionary if you can't	choose texts with useful information.
4. Underline keywords so that you can	put ideas into English word for word.
5. When you take notes, only	find them again easily.
6. If you are using a German text, don't	guess important new words.

b) *Now look on the Internet or in books and brochures. Get the information you need for your part of the project. Also collect anything else you might need: maps, photos, charts etc.*

4 Prepare your presentation *(Lösungen S. 92)*

a) *Here are different steps that can help you to prepare for a presentation. Decide on the best order:*

B → C → E → A → F → D

A: *Make handouts for your audience (new words, …)*
B: *Check that all the work has been done.*
C: *Decide the order you will give the information in.*
D: *Practise and check how long the presentation takes.*
E: *Write notes you can use when you talk.*
F: *Get any equipment you need (CD player, …)*

b) *Sort these presentation phrases under the headings 'Introduction', 'Main part', 'End'.*

- In this part we want to tell you about …
- That brings us to the end.
- The topic of our presentation is …
- As you can see on the map, …
- Now we're going to show you …
- We hope you enjoyed it.
- The presentation will have … parts.
- Thank you for your attention.
- You can ask questions at the end.

5 Practise and give your presentation

Practise and help each other to improve. Then give your presentation in class. Don't forget to allow time for questions at the end. (Maybe you can make a little quiz for your audience.)

TIP
- Give everyone in the group something to do.
- Speak slowly and clearly.
- Try not to look at your notes all the time.
- Use pictures to give information, too.

⟨A Puzzle⟩ The logic[1] puzzle

Julie, David, Mark and Chloe sit next to each other in class. They are all interested in different things. What is their favourite sport, food, country, film and colour? Complete the chart. You can get all the information you need from the clues[2]. Read through the clues several[3] times. You will be able to get more information every time you reread them. Logic skills are everything you need. GOOD LUCK!

	1	2	3	4
Name	Mark	Julie	David	Chloe
Sport	skateboarding	athletics	rugby	tennis
Food	vegetables	noodles	fish and chips	pizza
Country	Egypt	Japan	Australia	Finland
Film	thriller	science fiction	action	love story
Colour	blue	green	red	yellow

Names: Julie, David, Mark, Chloe
Sports: skateboarding, tennis, rugby, athletics
Food: noodles, pizza, fish and chips, vegetables
Countries: Egypt, Japan, Australia, Finland
Films: science fiction, action, thriller, love story
Colours: red, blue, green, yellow

Clues:

1. The person who plays tennis likes to watch love stories.
2. Mark likes skateboarding and only has a neighbour to his right.
3. David sits to the right of the person who would like to travel to Japan.
4. Julie sits next to Mark and doesn't like tennis.
5. The person who sits on the third chair likes rugby.
6. Mark sits next to the person whose favourite colour is green.
7. David would like to visit Australia, but he doesn't enjoy love stories.
8. The person whose favourite food are vegetables likes to watch thrillers.
9. Chloe sits next to the person who likes action films.
10. Julie loves to watch science fiction films.
11. The neighbour of the person whose favourite colour is red would like to visit Finland.
12. Chloe doesn't like fish and chips.
13. The person who loves noodles sits next to the person who would like to visit Egypt.
14. The person whose favourite colour is blue doesn't like love stories.

[1]**logic** ['lɒdʒɪk] = Logik • [2]**clue** [klu:] = Hinweis, Tipp • [3]**several** ['sevrl] = einige, mehrere

List of irregular verbs

infinitive	simple past	past participle	German
to **be** [bi:]	**was / were** [wɒz, wɜ:]	**been** [bi:n]	sein
to **become** [bɪ'kʌm]	**became** [bɪ'keɪm]	**become** [bɪ'kʌm]	werden
to **bleed** [bli:d]	**bled** [bled]	**bled** [bled]	bluten
to **break** [breɪk]	**broke** [brəʊk]	**broken** ['brəʊkn]	(zer)brechen; kaputtmachen
to **bring** [brɪŋ]	**brought** [brɔ:t]	**brought** [brɔ:t]	(mit)bringen
to **build** [bɪld]	**built** [bɪlt]	**built** [bɪlt]	bauen
to **burn** [bɜ:n]	**burnt / burned** [bɜ:nt, bɜ:nd]	**burnt / burned** [bɜ:nt, bɜ:nd]	(ver)brennen
to **buy** [baɪ]	**bought** [bɔ:t]	**bought** [bɔ:t]	kaufen
to **catch** [kætʃ]	**caught** [kɔ:t]	**caught** [kɔ:t]	fangen
to **choose** [tʃu:z]	**chose** [tʃəʊz]	**chosen** ['tʃəʊzn]	(aus)wählen
to **come** [kʌm]	**came** [keɪm]	**come** [kʌm]	kommen
to **cost** [kɒst]	**cost** [kɒst]	**cost** [kɒst]	kosten
to **deal** (with) [di:l]	**dealt** [dealt]	**dealt** [dealt]	(be)handeln
to **do** [du:]	**did** [dɪd]	**done** [dʌn]	machen, tun
to **draw** [drɔ:]	**drew** [dru:]	**drawn** [drɔ:n]	zeichnen
to **drink** [drɪŋk]	**drank** [dræŋk]	**drunk** [drʌŋk]	trinken
to **drive** [draɪv]	**drove** [drəʊv]	**driven** ['drɪvn]	fahren
to **eat** [i:t]	**ate** [et, eɪt]	**eaten** ['i:tn]	essen
to **fall** [fɔ:l]	**fell** [fel]	**fallen** ['fɔ:lən]	(herunter)fallen, hinfallen
to **feed** [fi:d]	**fed** [fed]	**fed** [fed]	füttern
to **feel** [fi:l]	**felt** [felt]	**felt** [felt]	(sich) fühlen
to **fight** [faɪt]	**fought** [fɔ:t]	**fought** [fɔ:t]	kämpfen, (sich) streiten
to **find** [faɪnd]	**found** [faʊnd]	**found** [faʊnd]	finden
to **fly** [flaɪ]	**flew** [flu:]	**flown** [fləʊn]	fliegen
to **forget** [fə'get]	**forgot** [fə'gɒt]	**forgotten** [fə'gɒtn]	vergessen
to **get** [get]	**got** [gɒt]	**got** [gɒt]	holen, bringen; (be)kommen; werden
to **give** [gɪv]	**gave** [geɪv]	**given** ['gɪvn]	geben
to **go** [gəʊ]	**went** [went]	**gone** [gɒn]	gehen
to **grow** [grəʊ]	**grew** [gru:]	**grown** [grəʊn]	wachsen
to **hang** [hæŋ]	**hung** [hʌŋ]	**hung** [hʌŋ]	hängen
to **have** [hæv]	**had** [hæd]	**had** [hæd]	haben
to **hear** [hɪə]	**heard** [hɜ:d]	**heard** [hɜ:d]	hören
to **hide** [haɪd]	**hid** [hɪd]	**hidden** ['hɪdn]	(sich) verstecken
to **hit** [hɪt]	**hit** [hɪt]	**hit** [hɪt]	schlagen; treffen
to **hold** [həʊld]	**held** [held]	**held** [held]	halten
to **hurt** [hɜ:t]	**hurt** [hɜ:t]	**hurt** [hɜ:t]	verletzen, weh tun
to **keep** [ki:p]	**kept** [kept]	**kept** [kept]	behalten
to **know** [nəʊ]	**knew** [nju:]	**known** [nəʊn]	wissen; kennen
to **lay** [leɪ]	**laid** [leɪd]	**laid** [leɪd]	legen
to **learn** [lɜ:n]	**learnt/learned** [lɜ:nt, lɜ:nd]	**learnt/learned** [lɜ:nt, lɜ:nd]	lernen
to **leave** [li:v]	**left** [left]	**left** [left]	(ver)lassen, abfahren

infinitive	simple past	past participle	German
to **lend** [lend]	**lent** [lent]	**lent** [lent]	leihen
to **let** [let]	**let** [let]	**let** [let]	lassen
to **lose** [lu:z]	**lost** [lɒst]	**lost** [lɒst]	verlieren
to **make** [meɪk]	**made** [meɪd]	**made** [meɪd]	machen, tun
to **mean** [mi:n]	**meant** [ment]	**meant** [ment]	bedeuten; meinen
to **meet** [mi:t]	**met** [met]	**met** [met]	(sich) treffen
to **pay** [peɪ]	**paid** [peɪd]	**paid** [peɪd]	(be)zahlen
to **put** [pʊt]	**put** [pʊt]	**put** [pʊt]	setzen, stellen, legen
to **read** [ri:d]	**read** [red]	**read** [red]	lesen
to **ride** [raɪd]	**rode** [rəʊd]	**ridden** ['rɪdn]	fahren, reiten
to **ring** [rɪŋ]	**rang** [ræŋ]	**rung** [rʌŋ]	klingeln, läuten
to **run** [rʌn]	**ran** [ræn]	**run** [rʌn]	rennen, laufen
to **say** [seɪ]	**said** [sed]	**said** [sed]	sagen
to **see** [si:]	**saw** [sɒ:]	**seen** [si:n]	sehen
to **sell** [sel]	**sold** [səʊld]	**sold** [səʊld]	verkaufen
to **send** [send]	**sent** [sent]	**sent** [sent]	schicken
to **shake** [ʃeɪk]	**shook** [ʃʊk]	**shaken** ['ʃeɪkn]	schütteln
to **shine** [ʃaɪn]	**shone** [ʃɒn]	**shone** [ʃɒn]	scheinen; glänzen
to **shoot** [ʃu:t]	**shot** [ʃɒt]	**shot** [ʃɒt]	schießen
to **show** [ʃəʊ]	**showed** [ʃəʊd]	**shown** [ʃəʊn]	zeigen
to **sing** [sɪŋ]	**sang** [sæŋ]	**sung** [sʌŋ]	singen
to **sink** [sɪŋk]	**sank** [sæŋk]	**sunk** [sʌŋk]	sinken
to **sit** [sɪt]	**sat** [sæt]	**sat** [sæt]	sitzen
to **sleep** [sli:p]	**slept** [slept]	**slept** [slept]	schlafen
to **slide** [slaɪd]	**slid** [slɪd]	**slid** [slɪd]	rutschen; gleiten
to **smell** [smel]	**smelt/smelled** [smelt, smeld]	**smelt/smelled** [smelt, smeld]	riechen
to **speak** [spi:k]	**spoke** [spəʊk]	**spoken** ['spəʊkn]	sprechen
to **spend** [spend]	**spent** [spent]	**spent** [spent]	ausgeben; verbringen
to **stand** [stænd]	**stood** [stʊd]	**stood** [stʊd]	stehen
to **steal** [sti:l]	**stole** [stəʊl]	**stolen** ['stəʊlən]	stehlen
to **swim** [swɪm]	**swam** [swæm]	**swum** [swʌm]	schwimmen
to **take** [teɪk]	**took** [tʊk]	**taken** ['teɪkn]	(mit)nehmen, bringen
to **teach** [ti:tʃ]	**taught** [tɔ:t]	**taught** [tɔ:t]	lehren
to **tell** [tel]	**told** [təʊld]	**told** [təʊld]	erzählen, sagen
to **think** [θɪŋk]	**thought** [θɔ:t]	**thought** [θɔ:t]	denken, glauben
to **throw** [θrəʊ]	**threw** [θru:]	**thrown** [θrəʊn]	werfen
to **understand** [ˌʌndə'stænd]	**understood** [ˌʌndə'stʊd]	**understood** [ˌʌndə'stʊd]	verstehen
to **wake** [weɪk]	**woke** [wəʊk]	**woken** ['wəʊkn]	(auf)wecken; (auf)wachen
to **wear** [weə]	**wore** [wɔ:]	**worn** [wɔ:n]	anhaben, tragen
to **win** [wɪn]	**won** [wʌn]	**won** [wʌn]	gewinnen, siegen
to **write** [raɪt]	**wrote** [rəʊt]	**written** ['rɪtn]	schreiben

Weitere Lösungen und Erwartungshorizonte (EH)

Unit 1

Page 4 ex. 1b) ***(Erwartungshorizont)***

1. In rugby the players kick or carry an oval ball. They play on a grass pitch.
2. In tennis the players use a racket to hit the ball. The umpire sits on a tall chair.
3. Cricket matches can go on for five days. The players play with a bat.
4. Skateboarders jump and do tricks in the air. They wear helmets for their heads.
5. There are 11 players in a football team. A match is 90 minutes long.
6. In athletics you run, jump or throw. An athletics track is 400 metres long.

Page 6 ex. 9 ***(Erwartungshorizont)***

1. Will you wash my football clothes, please?
2. I'll get your kite.
3. Will someone help me, please?
4. I'll open the door for you.

Page 8 ex. 14b) ***(Erwartungshorizont)***

1. … likes people who are interested in sports.
2. … likes books which are funny.
3. …likes games that you can play with a lot of friends.
4. … doesn't like people who are only interested in football.
5. … doesn't like clothes that are too expensive.
6. … doesn't like stars who get angry when they lose a match.

Page 9 ex. 17 ***(Erwartungshorizont)***

a) bird: landed on court, stood there, didn't want to leave, ball kid chased it away, bird flew up into air again
racket: player made bad mistakes, gave racket to ball kid, took place of ball kid, joke
umpire: ball hit umpire on head, almost fell out of his chair, not funny, headache

b) Today a bird landed on the tennis court. It stood there and didn't want to leave. The ball kid chased it away and then it flew up into the air again. One tennis player made many bad mistakes in the match. He gave the ball kid his racket and took her place as a ball kid. He also hit the umpire on the head with the ball. The umpire almost fell out of his chair. The umpire didn't think it was funny. Maybe he got a headache.

Page 10 ex. 20 ***(Erwartungshorizont)***

Last Sunday Matthew, Paul and Daniel were having fun. They were playing football in the garden and were enjoying the game a lot. But a neighbour was watching them from her own garden. She got angry and told the boys to stop. She pointed to a sign which said 'no ball games'. But Matthew had a brilliant idea … and so the boys played football with an empty tin!

Page 11 ex. 23

1. Ja, der Klub hat seinen eigenen Skatepark.
2. Ja, man kann auch als Anfänger/-in Mitglied werden.
3. Information nicht im Text.
4. Reduzierte Preise bei bestimmten Skateboard-Geschäften.
5. Ja, es gibt auch Sicherheitstraining.
6. Sie meinen, dass Skateboarden nicht nur ein Hobby ist, sondern auch eine Kunstform und eine Art und Weise, sich fortzubewegen.

Unit 2

Page 15 ex. 1c) ***(Erwartungshorizont)***

2. William the Conqueror defeated Harold at the Battle of Hastings in 1066.
3. The Saxons hated the Normans.
4. Queen Elizabeth I wanted to make England stronger and richer than Spain.
5. The Industrial Revolution started in England in the 18th century.
6. Britain was very rich when Victoria was Queen of England.
7. There are a lot of countries in the European Union.

Page 16 ex. 4b)

1. Matt isn't allowed to take photos in the theatre.
2. Sue isn't able to understand Russian.
3. Every pupil is allowed to borrow two books from the library.
4. Jack isn't able to go to the concert without a ticket.
5. Amy is able to swim 50 metres under water.

Page 19 ex. 10b) ***(Erwartungshorizont)***

I would like to visit a technology museum.

1. Can you tell me where the steam engines are, please?
2. May I take a photo of this machine?
3. How old is this machine?
4. How does it work?
5. Where can I get postcards and brochures?

Page 22 ex. 15 ***(Erwartungshorizont)***

B *Who:* Hanna Todd • *When*: In 1837; • *Where:* The Lonsdale Factory, Manchester • *What:* Job in factory

C b) 1827: born in London • 1833: father dies, family goes into workhouse • 1837: starts to work in factory near Manchester, lives with other children in big house near factory • 1845: leaves house, gets better job at the factory • 1850: leaves Lonsdale factory • 1870: dies

D a) Hannah Todd worked very hard. She had a sad life because her family was so poor. Hannah was scared when a man took her to Lonsdale factory, but her mother told her she would have a better life there. She worked hard for many years. Hannah was a clever girl and learnt how to be safe in the factory.

Page 23 ex. 17 ***(Erwartungshorizont)***

10 June 2006: Today I found my great-grandmother's diary. In the 19th century she worked as a servant in a large Victorian house. Her story is very interesting. It was hard for her because she missed her family but

she made friends with Timothy, a boy who was the same age as her. Timothy had visions, he had the sixth sense!
15 March 2007: I've read the rest of the diary now. I went to the town library to check if Timothy's visions were true. They were! I found an article in the local newspaper about Lady Cumberland's son who died in India. Timothy also had a vision about a girl called Chloe and a boy called Clarence. They have an accident in a flying machine and Chloe dies. I'm glad Chloe's boyfriend is called Alex!
25 April 2007: Chloe told me today that her class are going on a school trip to Spain. I'm scared because they are going to go by plane. I don't want to talk about that trip.
6th May 2007: Today was a terrible day. Chloe found the diary and started to read it. When she told her boyfriend Alex about the story, he said that his real name was Clarence! I don't want Chloe to see him anymore. We left London and went to stay with my sister in Manchester for a while. I phoned Alex's mother to explain to her why we left. Chloe was sad but she understood that it's better this way. I'm not sure whether Alex understands.

Revision for tests Unit 1–2

Page 26 ex. 2 *(Erwartungshorizont)*

Good idea: chance to try new sports; fun; chance to be outside
Bad idea: dangerous; expensive; no fun when the weather is bad

Hi everyone! I read the article about P.E. in last month's school magazine and found it very interesting. I agree that it would be great fun to try out new sports in P.E. like skateboarding or orienteering. Of course, if the weather was bad, we would have to stay in the school, but we could do sports outside in good weather. I don't think it's true that we wouldn't have time for other sports like football, volleyball and swimming. We could do the new sports only once a month, for example. Of course, skateboarding, in-line skating, orienteering, climbing or golf would be more expensive because we would have to buy the equipment. But maybe we could collect money in a school sale and share the equipment with other classes. Robert

Page 27 ex. 4 *(Erwartungshorizont)*

a) 1. battle, ships, Nelson, Trafalgar Square, Nelson's Column
   2. I think the text is about a battle at sea which happened a long time ago. I think many men were killed or hurt in the battle.

b) The text is about the battle of Trafalgar. It happened on 21st October 1805. It happened near Cape Trafalgar on the Spanish coast. Nelson defeated the Spanish and the French.

c) 1. The important people in the text are Admiral Villeneuve, Lord Nelson, Lieutenant Pasco and Captain Hardy.
   2. 21st October 1805, 8 am: French ship sees British ships near Cape Trafalgar; Nelson tells Pasco to send signal to British ships • after 10 am: Battle of Trafalgar begins • 1.15 pm: Nelson is shot in the shoulder • 4.30 pm: Nelson dies

d) 1. Dear Lady Hamilton, I have been with Nelson at sea for a very long time. I am very sorry to tell you that he was shot in the battle yesterday and died. He spoke to me about you and your daughter Horatia and wanted his friends to look after you. He was a great man and a wonderful admiral. I told him that we had won the battle before he died. He was very happy because he had done his duty. His last sea battle was very important for England because we defeated the enemy. Captain Hardy
   2. I can see a lot of smoke from the ships. The smoke has a strong smell. Men are hurt and are dying all around me. They are in pain and are screaming very loudly. There is blood and water and there are dead bodies on the ship. The battle is very noisy, the shots are very loud. People are shouting in many different languages.

Unit 3

Page 28 ex. 2b) *(Erwartungshorizont)*

Sarah, can u meet me 2moro after school? Tom and Jamie will b there 2 ;-)

Page 28 ex. 3 *(Erwartungshorizont)*

I'm glad that I don't have to share a room. I really like it when my aunt comes to visit us. I sometimes get fed up when my older brother gets more pocket money than I do. It's so embarrassing when my father sings.

Page 30 ex. 9 *(Erwartungshorizont)*

Es gibt eine Liste von Notfallnummern neben dem Telefon. Die Betriebsanleitungen für die elektrischen Geräte liegen auf dem Regal in der Küche. Die Mikrowelle funktioniert leider nicht. Die Müllabfuhr kommt dienstags. Die Nachbarn werden uns die Mülltrennung erklären. Wir können die Fahrräder, die in der Garage stehen, benutzen, aber wir sollen daran denken, auf der linken Seite zu fahren! Falls wir eine schwarze Katze sehen, sollen wir sie bitte nicht füttern. Sie wüschen uns viel Spaß in England und freuen sich auf Deutschland.

Page 33 ex. 16b)

2. If I were you, I would train him.
3. If I were you, I would use a dictionary.
4. If I were you, I would put up some nice posters.
5. If I were you, I would join some clubs.

Page 34 ex. 19

2. If you hadn't forgotten the cake, you wouldn't have burnt it.
3. If you had brought me your dirty clothes sooner, I would/could have washed them.
4. If you had played football in the garden, you wouldn't have broken the television.
5. If you hadn't tried to carry that heavy box alone, you wouldn't have hurt your back.
6. If I hadn't had a camera, I couldn't have taken the photograph.

Page 35 ex. 22a) ***(Erwartungshorizont)***

Hello, this is Sally Patterson. – Hello, Mrs Patterson, this is Nicola Green. I'd like to speak to Amy, please. – Sorry, she's not in at the moment, but she should be home soon. Can she call you back? – Oh, maybe I could just leave a message? – Of course. Just a moment, I'll get a pen ... – Could you please tell her I've got the flu and I can't go to the cinema with her tomorrow. – OK, I'll tell her. Get well soon, Nicola! – Thanks a lot, Mrs Patterson. Bye. – You're welcome. Bye!

Page 36 ex. 26 ***(Erwartungshorizont)***

a) sofa, television, video games, computer, snacks, games, posters, books, MP3 player, DVDs, table tennis table, phone ...
watch television, listen to music, play computer games, eat and drink, sleep, chat, relax ...
b) My dream room is very big. It has got a double bed and a sofa. There is a computer, a large TV and a DVD player. It is almost like a cinema. In my dream room I can also play table tennis with my friends. The walls are orange and green. There are lots of posters of my favourite bands on the walls. I have got a phone in my dream room so I can call my friends. We can play computer games at the weekend. I have got lots of chocolate and drinks in my room, too. My friends and I chat and relax there. We listen to loud music and sometimes have parties. My parents are not allowed to come into my room.

Unit 4

Page 40 ex. 3 ***(Erwartungshorizont)***

Dear Samuel, Today I am writing you a postcard from Kassel. The strong man you can see on this card is called "Hercules", and you can see him from many places in Kassel because he stands on top of a mountain. We have also got beautiful parks and a castle, and many museums. Yesterday I went to see the Kassel Huskies. They are our ice hockey team and I am their biggest fan. And they won the game! Would you like to come and visit me? See you soon, Leonhard

Page 45 ex. 14b) ***(Erwartungshorizont)***

Last week, my friend Linda and I had to do a presentation about the Royal Family. We had worked hard to prepare it, and we had practised at home, too, but we were still very nervous. When our teacher said "Lisa and Linda, please come to the blackboard and start your presentation" I did not feel well at all! But I felt better as soon as we had started, and in the end I even liked talking to the class. When we had finished, the other pupils applauded, and we felt great!

Page 47 ex. 17/3 ***(Erwartungshorizont)***

Oxford is a university town in the south of England. The university is over 750 years old. Students from all round the world go to Oxford – there is an exchange programme with the University of Tübingen in Baden-Württemberg, for example. Tourists can go on boat trips, visit old libraries and museums, have lunch in restaurants or go shopping. They can also learn a lot about Oxford's history by finding out interesting facts about the Romans, the Saxons, the Normans and about Richard the Lionheart. There are many different traditions on 1st of May: After May Day Singing there are breakfast picnics in the college gardens, and some crazy students jump into the River Cherwell.

Page 48 ex. 20c) ***(Erwartungshorizont)***

My favourite holiday town in the UK is Cardiff, the capital of Wales. This large and beautiful city on the south coast of the country is a great place for a summer holiday because there are many things to see and do. You can visit Cardiff Castle or the National Assembly for Wales. My dad loves operas, so he can go to the Welsh National Opera in the Wales Millennium Centre. My mum will be happy to visit the National Museum and Gallery, and my brother can watch a rugby match at the Millennium Stadium. The only thing that is not so good about a holiday in Cardiff is that we cannot be sure that the sun will shine!

Revision for tests Unit 3–4

Page 51 ex. 2 ***(Erwartungshorizont)***

a) Message a): *Who:* Shirin
What: go to the cinema
Where: the Riverside Film Centre
When: six o'clock tomorrow
Message b): *Who:* David
What: title of geography project
Where: at home
When: after 7
Message c): *Who:* Shirin
What: rehearsal for school play
Where: at school (?)
When: 5.30
b) Hi, this is Sarah. Sorry I can't answer my phone right now. Please leave a message and I'll call you back as soon as possible. Bye!

Page 51 ex. 3 ***(Erwartungshorizont)***

a) I would like to visit Edinburgh.
historical buildings, museums, festivals, concerts, restaurants
b) To whom it may concern,
I am a Year 7 pupil at ... School in Berlin. I am doing an English project called "Visit Britain" and I would like to get some information about Edinburgh.
I have read that Edinburgh is a beautiful city. What famous historical buildings can tourists visit? Which museums can you recommend? I have heard that there are good festivals in Edinburgh. Which festival would you recommend? What sort of concerts are on in the summer? Could you please give me the names of some good restaurants or other nice places to eat?
Could you please send me some brochures, too?
Thank you very much!
Sincerely, ...

Page 51 ex. 4 ***(Erwartungshorizont)***

1. Rhona: Shall I open the door for you?
Aunt Zeba: Yes, please. That's very kind of you.

2. Rhona: I'm terribly sorry!
Shirin: That's OK.
3. Boy: Can I help you?
Rhona: Could you show me how to get to Albert Dock, please?
4. Boy: Sorry.
Rhona: No problem. But be more careful next time.

Page 52 ex. 5 *(Erwartungshorizont)*

a) topic: Bhangra music
most important points: Bhangra popular in Britain and America, started in Pakistan and India, traditional instruments are the *tumbi* and the *dhol*, Kuldip Manak one of the most famous Bhangra singers, Bhangra is changing, is now multicultural music
b) musical instruments: *tumbi* (one string, difficult to play); *dhol* (a drum you hit with two sticks)
history: Bhangra started in Punjab region (west Pakistan and north-west India); farmers danced and sang Bhangra in the fields; later people sang songs at marriages, New Year and other festivals; Bhangra now popular all over the world; Bollywood films also made Bhangra popular
geography: started in Punjab region; now popular all over world (America, UK ...)
free time activities: no information in text
famous people: Kuldip Manak, father of modern Bhangra; Malkit Singh, popular Bhangra star
tourist industry: no information in text
c) 1. This week we are going to talk about and listen to Bhangra music. What exactly is Bhangra music? Well, it's a type of music which started in Pakistan and India but is now popular in Britain, America and all over the world. When we play the music, you will hear the two traditional instruments, the *tumbi* and the *dhol*. When it first began, Bhangra was the music of the farmers in the fields. Now it is played at marriages, New Year and other festivals. You might also have heard Bhangra in Bollywood films, which made Bhangra really popular. Now let's listen to some music by Kuldip Manak, a famous Bhangra musician.

Unit 5

Page 53 ex. 1 *(Testauswertung)*

1. a) = 4 b) = 6 c) = 2
2. a) = 6 b) = 4 c) = 2
3. a) = 2 b) = 4 c) = 6
4. a) = 2 b) = 6 c) = 4
5. a) = 6 b) = 4 c) = 2
6. a) = 4 b) = 2 c) = 6
7. a) = 2 b) = 4 c) = 6
8. a) = 4 b) = 6 c) = 2

16–26: You use some of the media sometimes, but your friends are more important to you. That's great – but be careful you don't miss the chances the high-tech media offer. This is the age of the Internet, you know!
27–39: You like the best of both worlds, don't you? All kinds of media are interesting for you, but you mix your media with friends and other hobbies. You have fun with the media, on the sports field – and even at school!
38–48: You spend a lot of time with the media, and TV characters are becoming more important than friends for you. (Maybe you're even in love with somebody from EastEnders!) Watch out!

Page 54 ex. 5

2. The knives and forks have been put on the tables.
3. A chair has been found for his/the director's assistant.
4. Everybody's make-up has been checked.
5. The door has been closed.
6. Gloria has been told her costume looks great.

Page 57 ex. 10 *(Erwartungshorizont)*

a) Eric's game: computer game – scary tiger, river – Eric – very excited – must finish for meal
"Holo-Comm": machine in his room – takes him to other worlds with monsters – Eric loves it
Calm-down belt: puts it on after game – helps him to relax/forget scary things – makes his room pink
b) Everything is pink because that colour helps to calm people down. It is the same in other people's homes.

Page 59 ex. 16a)

1. No, they're muesli bars. • They're healthy. • There are many different flavours.
2. No, he's going to be on stage. • Well, this is his last concert in Germany. • You can get tickets online or at the ticket office.
3. No, it's an ad for (polo) shirts. • No, you can get them in these six colours. • They were designed by Superstar Tommy.

Page 60 ex. 17b) *(Erwartungshorizont)*

Six cameras stolen in one hour
Yesterday afternoon six cameras were stolen in one hour from a large department store in the centre of town. A 15 year-old girl was caught outside by the police when she was leaving the store. She had stolen 6 cameras. The girl had been seen by a store assistant who called the police. Her bag and pockets were full of stolen things. The girl had had trouble with bullies at school. She had needed money and the cameras had been "ordered" by other thieves.
These clever thieves use teenagers who need money to steal things for them. Parents and schools don't know about this. Hundreds of cameras, mobile phones etc. are stolen every year. Sometimes they are sold on the Internet.
If you are bullied you can call this Helpline number: ... Don't buy stolen things! Buy things from shops, not from people you don't know. Check if the product box has been opened.

Page 61 ex. 20 *(Erwartungshorizont)*

The year is 2030. Ben's mother has just woken him up with the computer next to his bed because she is on holidays for the week, so she cannot wake him up herself. Ben turns the computer off so he can sleep for a few more minutes. After breakfast he goes into his home classroom, which is in his parents' house. He is alone in the classroom and he can see his teacher on a very big computer screen. The teacher can also see him and the other kids who are in their home classrooms. They practice writing on their mobile phones. Then they listen to a text on their MP3 players. In the text, the man talks about a time when kids wrote with pens on paper. Ben and the other pupils find this very funny. They have never learnt to write with a pen because they type everything on computers or mobile phones. After school, Ben plays a new interactive computer game with his friends. He can see and talk to his friends on the computer, too.

Page 63 ex. 26 *(Erwartungshorizont)*

Last Saturday a volleyball match against Highdale School was played. After the match, two mice were found in the school changing rooms by our volleyball team. One girl was very scared of the mice, but another girl really liked them, so they were brought to her house and they became her new pets.

Unit 6

Page 65 ex. 1

a) A – 3.; C – 2.; D – 1.
b) ***(EH)*** Frank: Sahara/Africa, 1989–1990, 1 year, camel • Isabella: Japan, 1878, some months, horse • Kyle: Canada, 2005–2006, 17 months, walk/ on foot
c) ***(EH)*** I think Frank Cole's journey would be scariest for me because crossing a desert is very dangerous. Crossing a desert alone must be scary because if you need help you have nobody to ask. If you don't have enough water you will die very soon. There are also thieves in the desert, and if you are alone they might steal your food and water and kill you. I would like to make the journey that Kyle Pickering made. I think Canada is a very beautiful country and if you travel across it in winter and summer you can see fantastic landscapes. I also think you would meet lots of interesting people on a journey like Kyle's.

Page 65 ex. 2b)

1. It takes 24 hours to fly from the UK to Australia.
2. It took Captain Cook 8 months to travel to Australia.
3. On Captain Cook's ship there was no fresh food.
4. Ryan is going to France next month.

Page 66 ex. 4b)

Dad said that the weather had been terrible the week before. He said it had been raining the day before and three days before it had been so windy that his hat had flown away. Dad said that that day the sun was shining and he was looking at the ocean just then. The next day he was travelling to Sydney to fly home and he said he would see us the following week.

Page 67 ex. 6

Du kannst vom Wassertaxi aus den Hafen anschauen. Das ist sehr erholsam.
Doch, du könntest Luna Park besuchen, wo es Fahrgeschäfte und Ausstellungen für die ganze Familie gibt.
Man kann eine Führung bis ganz nach oben machen, wenn man abenteuerlustig ist.
Ja, es gibt 30 Strände in Sydney, wo man baden, surfen oder die Sonne genießen kann.

Page 69 ex. 9b)

1. The police officer advises Ryan to leave the area.
2. Ryan asks what has happened.
3. The police officer explains that there has been a fire in the Webbs' house.
4. The police officer warns Ryan to move.
5. The police officer suggests to Ryan that he can find out more in the newspaper.

Page 69 ex. 11

1. The director told them to speak a bit more clearly.
2. The director told them to tell him about their dancing lessons.
3. The director told them not to sit on the cold floor.
4. The director told them to imagine they were princesses in a palace.
5. The director told them not to phone him every day the following week.

Page 70 ex. 13c) *(Erwartungshorizont)*

A: The fire service, please.
B: Where are you calling from?
A: Smiths' farm.
B: What's the problem?
A: A fire has started in a farm building.
B: Is there anybody inside?
A: No, but there are animals in there.
B: Ok, I'll send the fire service right away.
A: Thank you very much.

Page 72 ex. 19a) *(Erwartungshorizont)*

Everybody on the ship was scared. The Captain shouted: "Get the guns!" The pirate ship was getting closer. It was a very dangerous situation. The weather became very stormy. The ship was shaking in the waves. Brad decided to fight. He found a gun and stood up. That moment, a pirate shot at him. Brad fell to the ground, but he wasn't hurt. The bullet had hit the box the old man had given him. He got up again and shot at the pirates, who got scared, turned around and sailed away. Brad heard someone calling his name. Then the voice got louder. Suddenly, he woke up. It was his mother who said "Brad, I wish you wouldn't fall asleep over your homework!"

Revision for tests Unit 5–6

Page 75 ex. 1b)

1. Debbie said she had been very nervous before the interview the day before, but she was fine that evening.
2. Tom explained that the Casting Director was checking his script because she wanted him to play the role differently.
3. Anne said she was really super-happy. She had been chosen to act the role of Tracey.

Page 75 ex. 2b) ***(Erwartungshorizont)***

Britain's must-see places
A press conference about Britain's must-see places was held last Monday. Cornwall was the only place listed in the Lonely Planet's list of Britain's must-see places this year. The reasons given by the Lonely Planet were Cornwall's fantastic coast, beautiful landscape and its interesting history and culture.
A survey of tourists was done last year. The survey showed that tourists really liked the fresh farm food and fish used in pubs and the good swimming and surfing opportunities in the Atlantic. Other good points were the open-air theatre and concerts and old, the shops with traditional arts and crafts and the walks along coast paths.
For tourist information on Cornwall, check the website www.visitcornwall.co.uk. For surf news visit www.magicseaweed.com.

Page 76 ex. 3 ***(Erwartungshorizont)***

a) *Picture 1:* ambulance – old lady – fallen over – heavy shopping bags – holding her arm
Picture 2: police – burglar breaking into house
Picture 3: fire service – Greenburn Road – fire in room of house

b) 1. A: The ambulance service, please!
B: Where are you calling from?
A: Church Street.
B: What's the problem?
A: An old lady was on her way home. She was carrying heavy shopping bags and she has fallen over.
B: Is she hurt?
A: Yes, she's holding her arm.
B: OK, I'll send an ambulance right now.

2. A: I need the police, please!
B: Where are you calling from?
A: 17 Greenhill Road.
B: What has happened?
A: A burglar is breaking into a house.
B: How do you know?
A: I can see him from my flat.
B: I'll send the police right now.

3. A: The fire service, please! Quickly!
B: Where are you calling from?
A: I'm on Greenburn Road.
B: Where exactly is the fire?
A: 53 Greenburn Road.
B: Is anybody in the house?
A: I don't know. Please send the fire service as soon as possible.
B: They're on their way.

Page 76 ex. 4 ***(Erwartungshorizont)***

b) The author describes how Simon feels: "He was getting very excited and could feel the sweat on his hands". This shows that Simon is nervous and that something exciting is going to happen.
He uses short sentences: "No, it wasn't a game. It was more than that". / "Fast, then faster."
He gives the reader a shock: "… a warning suddenly flashed up on the screen: NOT FOR TEACHERS OR PARENTS!"

c) 1. Simon couldn't believe it. He could get an A in Maths if he looked at the test. He thought about it for a minute. Should he? Would it be very wrong? Should he show it to his friends, too? So many questions! Just then, his mother came into his room. She looked at the screen and asked "What's that?" Simon didn't know what to say. His mother read what was on the top of the page on the screen: "Maths test". She understood right away that it was not something Simon should see. She closed the screen, turned off the computer, and took the game away. 'Oh well then', thought Simon, 'I will have to study after all …!'
2. Teachers hate it, parents hate it, and kids love it! It's the new computer game called 'School Tricks'. If you have problems in Maths, English, or Geography, then this computer game can save your life! With this game, you can find copies of your school tests. All you need to do is click on the date and subject of your test in the main menu and find your test. It couldn't be easier!
3. Buy 'School Tricks' today! With this fantastic game, you'll never have problems in school again. Click on the date and subject of your test to see your test before the other students. Then you can see the questions and if you study, you will get an A, no problem. It couldn't be easier! Only 50 pounds!

Skills 1

Page 77 ex. 1a) ***(Erwartungshorizont)***

equestrian – Reit(er) – 2/4 • *calendar* – Kalender – 1/2 • *competitor* – Wettkampfgegner/-in – 3/4 • *(to) qualify* – (sich) qualifizieren – 1–4 • *rider* – Reiter – 1/3/4 • *arena* – Arena – 1/2/4 • *spectator* – Zuschauer/-in – 2/4 • *(to) take part* – teilnehmen – 4 • *fence* – *Hindernis* – 4 • *ton* – Tonne – 1/2 • *manure* – Mist – 4

Page 77 ex. 3

a) 1. Es wird eine neue Laufbahn für die Olympischen Spiele geben.
2. Der Zug hat etwas auf den Gleisen überfahren.
3. Die Fernsehkameras verfolgen den Ball das ganze Spiel lang.
4. Die Wanderer sind dem Weg in die Hügel/Berge gefolgt.
5. Der Reporter hat den Star in ihrem Hotel aufgespürt.
6. Am Telefon verliere ich oft die Zeit aus den Augen/vergesse ich oft die Zeit.

b) ***(Erwartungshorizont)***
1. There are a lot of cows in the farmer's field.
2. We played football on the school field.
3. He knows all about history. It's his field.
4. Smith fielded the ball well.

d) ***(Erwartungshorizont)***
1. Oh no, I've forgotten my Maths homework today. – That doesn't matter, we haven't got Maths today.

2. I think I'll use Sarah's bike. – You can't do that! You must ask her first.
3. Would you like some more? – Thanks, that's enough.
4. I did it! I got an A in my Geography test! – That's great. Well done!
5. My brother's rugby team lost the match. – That can't be true! They're the best team in England!
6. Ouch, I've hurt my knee! – Let's have a look. Oh dear, it's bleeding.

Skills 2

Page 78 ex. 1 *(Erwartungshorizont)*

1. Who is the lady on the horse?
2. When did she live?
3. What kind of person was she?
4. Where did she live?
5. Why is she famous?

Page 78 ex. 3 *(Erwartungshorizont)*

b) 1. The lady on the horse is Lady Godiva, the wife of Leofric, a lord.
2. She lived in the 11th century. She died in 1067.
3. She was a kind, gentle, shy and religious person.
4. She lived in Coventry.
5. She is famous because she rode through Coventry on a horse without any clothes so that her husband would be fair to the people of Coventry.

c) *before:* hard man, took money from poor people, strict with the Church
after: much kinder person, fair to people, gave money to the Church

Skills 3

Page 79 ex. 3a)

Message for Ed: three • Message for Lisa: 40

Skills 4

Page 80 ex. 3a)

1. Lincolnshire is in the east of England.
2. Vegetables and flowers grow in the Fens.
3. 'The Wolds' means open land.
4. Grimsby is famous for fish.
5. Thirteen towns have Farmers Markets.
6. The 'Tastes of Lincolnshire' sign tells you that there is regional food on the menu.

Skills 5

Page 81 ex. 2 *(Erwartungshorizont)*

Teenagers make a difference in Victoria Park
Victoria Park now looks great, thanks to the H15 Youth Club.
Last Saturday, a big group of teenagers met in the park and collected all the rubbish. More than 20 girls and boys worked all day. There had been lots of rubbish everywhere. It had been left on paths and on the grass. People had left all kinds of rubbish, such as paper and glass. First, everything was sorted into different bags, then it was taken away for recycling.
It was a hard job for Grace Adams, aged 16, and a wet job, too. "I got a broken skateboard and an old shoe out of the lake!" she said happily.
After many hours, the park was clean again. The young workers were tired but proud of their work. They felt they had made a real difference. The teenagers hope that in the future people will look after the park. Harry Nelson, aged 15, said "Please take your rubbish home with you".

Page 81 ex. 4 *(Erwartungshorizont)*

Event 1

b) *Who:* a group of teenagers, two boys and two girls, aged 15–16 • *Where:* on the street, in a big city, outside shops • *When:* Saturday afternoon • *Why:* to make some extra money to go on holidays • *What:* busking, playing instruments and singing

c) Group of teenagers – needed money for summer holidays – decided to go busking – practised at home – went into the city centre – brought instruments – busy street – nice weather – lots of people – stop, watch, listen, clap – give money – teenagers – very happy – more pocket money to go to summer camp

d) Teenagers sing and play music for holiday money
Last Saturday, a group of teenagers played music in the city centre. The group of two boys and two girls, aged between 15 and 16, thought of the idea when they wanted to make more pocket money to go to a summer camp for their holidays. Before they went busking, they practised at home. Peter, aged 16, said "We wanted to be good enough to play on a busy street".
On Saturday morning they brought their instruments to the street where all the big shops are and began to play. There were a lot of people in the city centre that day because of the nice weather. When they came out of the shops, many people stopped to listen to the teenagers. Everybody thought they were very good. They clapped and then they gave them money.
The teenagers earned over £100 and were very happy with the day. They now have enough pocket money to go to the summer camp for a week during their holidays.

Event 2

b) *Who:* a group of teenagers, boys and girls, aged 13–17 • *Where:* in the mountains • *When:* last Sunday • *Why:* raise money for charity • *What:* a 20 mile bike ride and picnic

c) Last Sunday – group of teenagers, aged 13–17 – mass bike ride – organised by teenagers for charity – plan event – posters – meeting at 10 am at school – everybody bring lunch and wear helmet – 20 miles in the mountains – difficult – after 10 miles picnic – weather very nice – lucky – 125 teenagers went on bike ride – one small accident – one boy, not badly hurt – success – raised money for charity

d) Charity Bike Ride
Last month a group of teenagers decided to organise a mass bike ride for charity. They spent a lot of time with the organisation of the event. First they made posters so everyone would know what was happening. Then they asked everyone to meet at the school at 10 o'clock on Sunday morning. Everybody had to bring a bike, something to eat and drink and a helmet. When everybody had arrived, they cycled to the mountains.
There were 125 teenagers, aged between 13 and 17, and the ride was 20 miles long. It was quite difficult for some of the teenagers. After 10 miles they stopped and had a picnic. They were lucky because the weather was quite warm and sunny. Everybody had fun on the ride. There was only one small accident, when a boy fell off his bike, but he wasn't badly hurt. The group raised a lot of money for a local charity and everybody was very happy about the success of the bike ride.

Event 3

b) *Who:* a group of students, boys and girls, aged 13–15 • *Where:* in the school hall • *When:* during the break • *Why:* to raise money for a new sports centre • *What:* a cake sale

c) School needs money for new sports centre – old centre too small – group of students – idea to have a cake sale in school hall – during break – everyone bake something – cake, bread – sell to teachers and other pupils – make money for sports centre – everyone had fun – headmaster – happy

d) School cake sale a success
Last week a group of teenagers decided to raise money for the new sports centre in the school. The old sports centre is too small so they have to build a new one. Some teachers asked the pupils to think of ways to raise money so one class decided to have a cake sale.
On Thursday evening everyone baked something at home. Some pupils baked cakes and others baked bread. On Friday they had the cake sale in the school hall during the break. The pupils took turns selling the cakes. Many teachers came to buy cake to have with their coffee and the other pupils were very happy that the cake sale had been organised.
After the cake sale Lisa, one of the pupils, said: "We really enjoyed the project! We've raised £200 for the new sports centre and we've all had fun, too". The headmaster was very happy that the cake sale was such a success and said that he was proud of the pupils.

Skills 6

Page 82 ex. 4b) *(Erwartungshorizont)*

Introduction: The topic of our presentation is … / The presentation will have … parts. / You will be able to ask questions at the end.
Main part: In this part we want to tell you about … / As you can see on the map, … / Now we're going to show you …
End: That brings us to the end. / We hope you enjoyed it. / Thank you for your attention.

Bildquellen:
U1/U4: Corbis/Skelley; S. 9: Picture-Alliance/Bibby; S. 12: shutterstock/RF/McNally; S. 14: MEV; S. 16: Avenue Images GmbH/Stockbyte; S. 21: Corel Corporation; S. 22: shutterstock/RF/ChipPix; S. 26: Marco Polo Agence Photographique/Naudin; S. 27: AKG; S. 32: Klett-Archiv/Hill; S. 41: Fotosearch RF/Photodisc; S. 44: Alamy Images RM/Image State; S. 47: Dinkhauser Kartonagen GmbH/Geiger; S. 52: (1) Wikimedia Foundation Inc./GNU/van der Crabben; (2) Yahoo! Deutschland GmbH/Badwhar; (3) Alamy Images RM/Noronha; S. 58: Avenue Images GmbH/image 100; S. 60: Mauritius/Pöhlmann; S. 64: Action Press/Rex; S. 67: Fotosearch RF/Brand X Pictures; S. 71: CartoonStock/McNeill; S. 74: Klett-Archiv/Reinke; S. 78: Corbis/Griffiths Belt; S. 79: Avenue Images GmbH/Stock Disc; S. 80: Alamy Images RF/Furlong; Portfolio: NewsCast

Textquellen:
S. 14: © Anthony Horowitz, Penguin 2002; S. 39: © Lemony Snicket, Harper Collins Children's Books; S. 64: © Joyce Carol Oates, Harper Collins Children's Books